NEW
PLACE NAMES
OF THE
WORLD

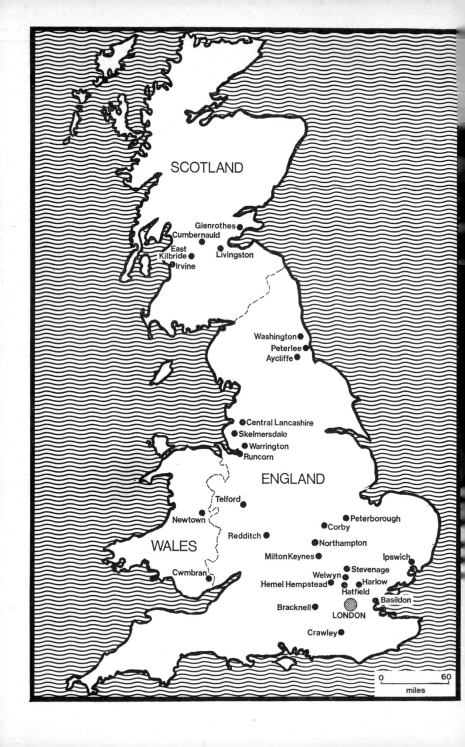

SCOTLAND

Glenrothes
Cumbernauld
East
Kilbride
Irvine
Livingston

Washington
Peterlee
Aycliffe

Central Lancashire
Skelmersdalo
Warrington
Runcorn

ENGLAND

Telford

Newtown

Redditch

WALES

Cwmbran

Peterborough
Corby
Northampton
MiltonKeynes
Ipswich
Welwyn Stevenage
Hemel Hempstead Harlow
Hatfield
Bracknell
Basildon
LONDON
Crawley

0   60
miles

NEW
PLACE NAMES
OF THE
WORLD

Hebe Spaull

author of "The New ABC of Civics",
"Africa: Continent on the Move",
"The World's Changed Face Since 1945", etc.

WARD LOCK LTD

LONDON and SYDNEY

SBN 7063 1057 8

Ward Lock Limited, 116 Baker Street
London WIM 2BB

*Made and printed in Great Britain
by Richard Clay (The Chaucer Press), Ltd.
Bungay, Suffolk*

AUTHOR'S NOTE

This book lists names of new towns and other places, such as artificial lakes, that have been created since 1945. It also lists those places whose names—and in some cases, national boundaries—have changed since then. In the latter case the names are listed both under their new and under their old names.

The author hopes that the book will prove especially useful to teachers of geography and also to business executives and professional people with overseas interests.

HEBE SPAULL

MAPS

A

ACRE, new State, central Brazil. Formerly a federal territory.

ACRE, seaport, Israel. Now Akko.

AFARS and ISSAS, French Territory of, N.E. coast of Africa. Formerly French Somaliland, renamed 1967. Capital: Jibouti.

AFULA, Israel. New town S. of Nazareth.

AHMEDI, Yemen. New deep seaport near Hodeida.

AJKA, Hungary. New industrial town, N. of Lake Balaton, centred round aluminium plant.

AKKO, Israel. Seaport. Formerly Acre.

AKOSOMBO, Ghana. New town and port around Lake Volta. Planned pop.: 50,000.

AKROTIRI, Cyprus. British sovereign area within the republic of Cyprus.

ALBERTVILLE, Congolese Republic. Now Kalemie.

ALEXANDROVSK, Sakhalin, Soviet Union, chief town. Formerly Japan.

ALLANRIDGE, South Africa, Orange Free State. Developed since 1945 as gold-mining town.

ALLENSTEIN, Germany. Now Olsztyn, Poland.

ALTHEIDE, Germany. Now Polanica Zdroj, Poland.

AMAPA, Brazil. New federal territory, N.E. Brazil.

ANDRHRA PRADESH. New Indian State, formed in 1956 by joining Telugu-speaking parts of Madras State with the Telegana area of Hyderabad State.

ANGERBURG, Germany. Now Wegorzewo, Poland.

ARAD, Israel. New town in Negev. Founded in 1962.

ARLITT, Niger. New town being built 600 miles N.E. of Niamey in connection with uranium mines in Southern Sahara.

ASHDOD, Israel. New port on Mediterranean Sea.

ASHGELON, Israel. New town near coast, N. of Gaza.

ATIKOKEN, Ont., Canada. Town built with development of Steep Rock iron-ore mines.

ATOMIC CITY, S.E. Idaho, U.S.A. Developed after 1949 with building of atomic reactor testing station.

AYCLIFFE, Durham, England. New Town founded 1947 near Darlington. Took name from small hamlet of sixty persons. Pop.: now 21,000.

B

BAD FLINSBERG, Germany. Now Swieradow Zroj, Poland.

BAD KUDOWA, Germany. Now Kudowa Zdroj, Poland.

BAD LANDECK, Germany. Now Ladek Zdroj, Poland.

BAD POLZIN, Germany. Now Polczyn Zdroj, Poland.

BAD REINERZ, Germany. Now Duszniki Zdroj, Poland.

BAD SALZBRUNN, Germany. Now Szczawno Zdroj, Poland.

BAD WARMBRUNN, Germany. Now Cieplica Slaskie Zdroj, Poland.

BAKAR, Yugoslavia. New port under construction on Adriatic.

BALAKA, Malawi. New town founded 1966 in south of country.

BANCROFT, Zambia. Now Chillapongwe.

BANDANDU, Congolese Republic. Formerly Banningville. Capital of province of same name.

BANNINGVILLE, Congolese Republic. Now Bandandu.

BANSKA BYSTRICA, Czechoslovakia. New region formed 1949 from part of central Slovakia. Capital is town of same name on R. Heron.

BARCE, East Libya. New town. Pop.: 11,000.

BARROW ISLAND, Western Australia. New oilfield.

BASILDON, Essex, England. New town founded 1949. Pop.: 77,200.

BASUTOLAND, now Lesotho.

BATAVIA, Indonesia, capital. Now Djakarta.

BAT YAM, Israel. New coastal town S. of Tel Aviv.

BECHUANALAND, now Botswana.

BECKERN, Germany. Now Piekary, Poland.

BE'ER SHEVA, Israel. New town, S.W. of Gaza.

BEIDA, Libya. New capital under construction in Cyranaica.

BEILAN, Germany. Now Pilawa, Poland.

BEISAN, town, Israel. Now Bet She'an.

BEJAIA, Constantine, Algeria. Seaport. Formerly Bougie. Connects with oil pipe-line to Massi-Messoud.

SOUTHERN AFRICA

CENTRAL AFRICA

NIGERIA

CAMEROON
Douala

EQUATORIAL GUINEA

GABON

CONGO
Brazzaville

CHAD

CENTRAL AFRICAN REPUBLIC

Issiro

Kishangani

Mbandaka

Bandandu
Kinshasha

SUDAN

ETHIOPIA
Addis Ababa

UGANDA
Kampala

CONGOLESE REPUBLIC

Mbuji–Mayi

Luanda

ANGOLA

SOMALIA
Mogadishu

KENYA
Nairobi
Mombasa

Kigali
RWANDA
BURUNDI
Bujumbura

TANZANIA
Dar es Salaam

Kalemie

Laikasi
Lubumbashi

ZAMBIA

Mtwara

Mbala
Mansa

400
miles
0

BELL BAY, Tasmania, Australia. At mouth of R. Tamar. Developed after 1949 with building of big aluminium plant.

BELOE ISLAND, New York Harbour, U.S.A. Now Liberty Island.

BENE BERAQ, Israel. New town, N.W. of Jerusalem.

BERKELEY, New South Wales, Australia. New town and steel centre, near Port Kembla.

BET SHE'AN, Israel. Town central Israel. Formerly Beisan.

BET SHEMESH, Israel. New town S.W. of Jerusalem.

BEITSCH, Germany. Now Biecz, Poland.

BELGARD, Germany. Now Bialogard, Poland.

BELGIAN CONGO. Now Congolese Republic (Kinshasa) or Democratic Republic of the Congo.

BENMORE LAKE, New Zealand. Created by dam on Waitaki R. North Otago. Has shoreline of 150 miles. Completed 1964.

BHADRAVATI, Mysore, India. New town.

BHAKRA-NANGAL CANAL, India. 2,700 miles long. Passes through three States.

BHUBANESWAR, new capital Orissa, India.

BIAFRA, name taken from Bight of Biafra and assumed by breakaway Eastern States of Nigeria (chiefly Ibo people) during Nigerian civil war. Ceased to exist, January 1970.

BIALOGARD, Lower Silesia, Poland. Formerly Belgard, Germany.

BIECZ, town, Lower Silesia, Poland. Formerly Beitsch, Germany.

BIERUTOWICE, town, Lower Silesia, Poland. Formerly Bruckenberg, Germany.

BINGERAU, Germany. Now Wegrow, Poland.

BIR MOGHREIN, town, Mauretania. Formerly Fort Trinquet.

BISCHDORF, Germany. Now Biskupin, Poland.

BISKUPIN, town, Lower Silesia, Poland. Formerly Bischdorf, Germany.

BLACHARNIA SLASKA, town, Upper Silesia, Poland. Formerly Blechhammer, Germany.

BLAGOYEVGRAD, chief town, Macedonia, Bulgaria. Formerly Gorna Dzhumaya.

BLECHHAMMER, Germany, town. Now Blacharnia Slaska, Upper Silesia, Poland.

11

BOLESLAWIEC, Lower Silesia, Poland, on Bobrawa River. Formerly Bunzlaw, Germany.

BOMI HILLS, district, Liberia. Developed after 1950.

BORNEO, Indonesia. Now Kalimantan.

BOSCHEKUL, Kazakistan, Soviet Union. Town founded 1968 to develop copper and molybdenum ores.

BOTSWANA, central African republic within British Commonwealth. Until 1966 British Protectorate of Bechuanaland. Area: 222,000 sq. miles. Pop.: 548,000. Cap.: Gaberones.

BOUGIE, Constantine, Algeria. Now Bejaia.

BOURBON, French island in Indian Ocean. Now Ile de Réunion.

BRACKNELL, Berks., England. New town 10 miles S. of Windsor. Pop.: 32,900. Founded in 1949.

BRASILIA, new city built as new capital of Brazil in what was the then State of Goia. 600 miles N.W. of Rio de Janeiro, former capital. Inaugurated 1960. Planned for pop. of 500,000.

BRASOV, Roumania, at foot of Transylvanian Alps. Formerly Stalin.

BREMERSDORP, Swaziland. Now Manzini.

BRENT, one of the new London boroughs, taken from river of same name. Comprises former municipal boroughs of Wembley and Willesden.

BRESLAU, Germany. Now Wroclaw, Poland.

BREST LITOVSK, Soviet Union. Town on frontier with Poland. Formerly Brezesc, Poland.

BRIEG, Germany. Now Brzeg, Poland.

BRITISH ANTARCTIC TERRITORY, created 1962 and comprising South Shetlands, South Orkneys and Graham Land. Total land area: 500,000 sq. miles. No permanent inhabitants.

BRITISH CAMEROONS. Since 1961 divided: northern part became part of Nigeria; southern part part of Federal Republic of Cameroon.

BRITISH GUIANA. Now Guyana.

BRITISH INDIAN OCEAN TERRITORY, created 1965. Consists of Chagos Archipelago and islands of Aldabra, Farquhar and Desroches. Pop.: about 1,400.

BRODNICA, town, near Danzig, Poland. Formerly Bruddenbrak, Germany.

EAST AFRICA

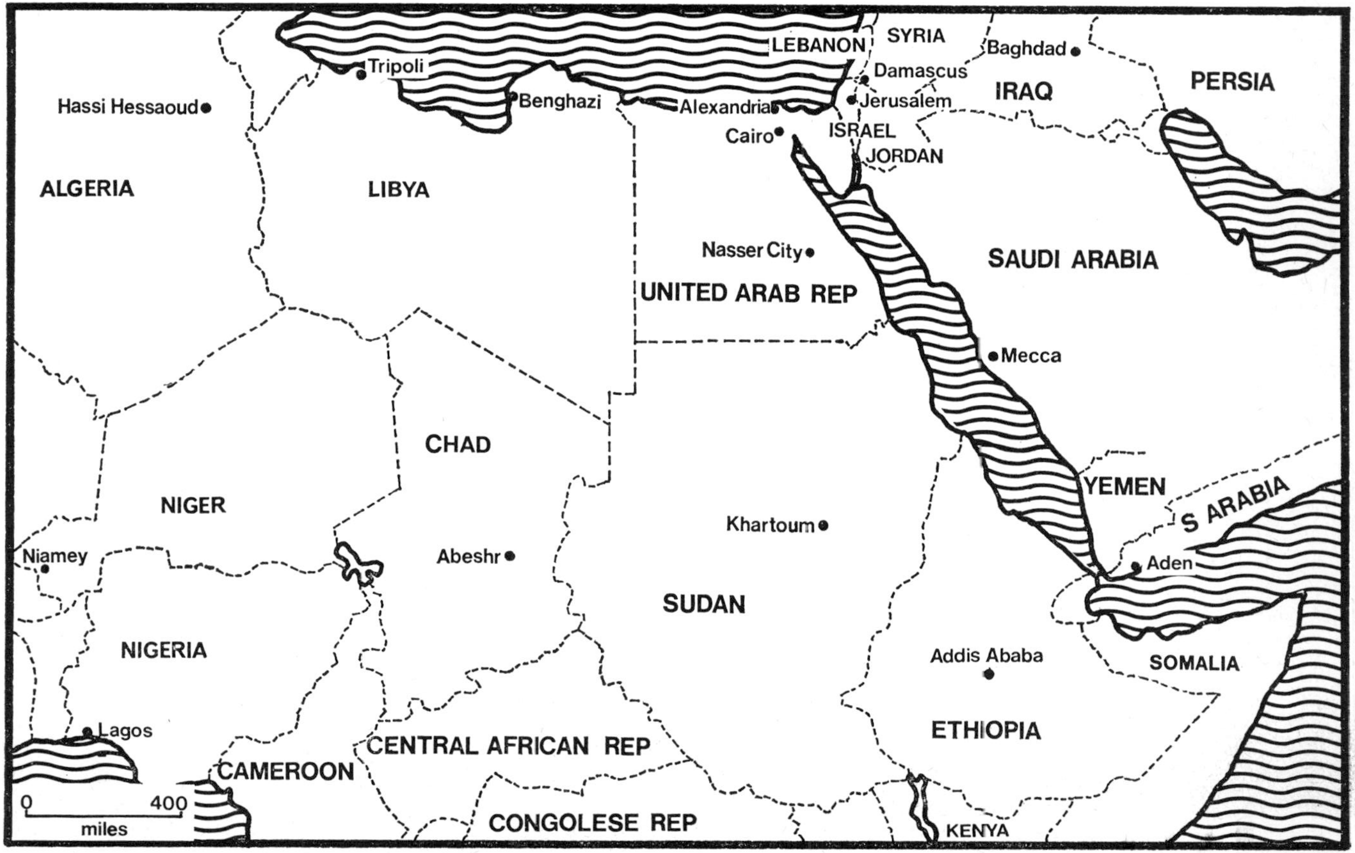
LEBANON
SYRIA
Baghdad
PERSIA
Tripoli
Damascus
IRAQ
Hassi Hessaoud
Benghazi
Alexandria
Jerusalem
Cairo
ISRAEL
JORDAN
ALGERIA
LIBYA
Nasser City
SAUDI ARABIA
UNITED ARAB REP
Mecca
CHAD
YEMEN
S ARABIA
NIGER
Khartoum
Niamey
Abeshr
Aden
SUDAN
NIGERIA
Addis Ababa
SOMALIA
Lagos
CENTRAL AFRICAN REP
ETHIOPIA
CAMEROON
0
400
miles
CONGOLESE REP
KENYA

BROKEN HILL, Zambia, Now Kabue.

BROKOPONDO LAKE, Surinam, South America. Covers about 700 sq. miles. Created by dam on Suriname R., where new aluminium smelter is under construction.

BRUDDENBRAK, Germany. Now Brodnica, Poland.

BRUKENBERG, Germany. Now Bierutowice, Poland.

BRZEG, Silesia, Poland, town on R. Oder. Formerly Brieg, Germany.

BUJUMBURA, capital of Burundi. Formerly Usumbura.

BUKHTARMA SEA, Soviet Union. Created by building dams on R. Dnieper. Stretches for about 370 miles.

BURGAN, Kuwait. Centre of oil production. Developed after 1946.

BURUNDI, independent State, central Africa on E. side of Lake Tanganyika. Was formerly part of Belgian trusteeship territory under United Nations of Ruanda-Urundi. Area: 10,747 sq. miles. Pop.: 3 millions. Cap.: Bujumbura.

BYRD LAND, Antarctica. Formerly Marie Byrd Land.

BYTOM, Upper Silesia, Poland. Formerly Beuthen, Germany.

C

CABORA BASA, Mozambique. Africa's largest artificial lake being created by dam here. By 1974 will be 1,000 miles long.

CALICUT, capital of Indian territory of Laccadive, Mincoy and Amindivi Islands. Now Kozhikode.

CAMBODIA, Kingdom, South-East Asia. Formerly part of French Indo-China. Became independent 1954–5. Area: 70,000 sq. miles. Pop.: 6,200,000. Cap.: Phnom-Penh, on Mekong R. Chief industries: rice and rubber.

CAMDEN, one of new London boroughs. It comprises the former boroughs of Hampstead, Holborn and St. Pancras. Name assumed in 1965.

CAMEROON, Federal Republic of, comprises the Eastern Cameroon, a former U.N. Trust Territory under French administration and Western Cameroon, part of U.N. Trust Territory under British administration. Area: 143,500 sq. miles. Pop.: 5,150,000. Cap.: Yaounde. Chief industries: cocoa, coffee and rubber.

CAPE CANAVERAL, U.S.A. Since 1963 Cape Kennedy.

CAPE KENNEDY, U.S.A. East Florida on Atlantic coast. Formerly Cape Canaveral.

CARLTONVILLE, Transvaal, South Africa. New town. Pop: 103,500.

CASEY STATION, Antarctica, near Wiles. Named 1969.

CAWNPORE, Uttar Pradesh, India. Now Kanpur.

CELEBES, island, Indonesia. Now Sulawesi.

CENTRAL AFRICAN REPUBLIC, formerly French colony of Ubanghi Shari. Became independent 1960. Area: 234,000 sq. miles. Pop.: 2,900,000. Cap.: Bangui, on R. Ubangi.

CENTRAL PROVINCES, India. Now Madhya Pradesh.

CERRO BOLIVAR, or Iron Mountain, Venezuela. Site of vast iron-ore deposits discovered 1948.

CHAD, republic of north-central Africa. Formerly part of French Equatorial Africa. Became independent 1960. Area: 467,920 sq. miles. Pop.: 3,400,000. Cap.: Fort Lamy (south of Lake Chad).

CHALNA, East Pakistan. New river port near new town of Khulna.

CHANDIGARH, India. New city, capital of the two States of Punjab and Hariana. Pop.: 90,000. The area was in 1966 constituted a Union Territory with the same name.

CHARANENTSAVAN, town, Armenia, Soviet Union. Formerly Lusavan.

CHEB, formerly Eger, Czechoslovakia.

CHEMNITZ, E. Germany. Now Karl-marx-stadt.

CHIIGIRIK, new town, Soviet Union, 21 miles south of Tashkent.

CHILLABONSWE, Zambia. Formerly Bancroft.

CHIMBOTE, Peru. Since 1950 has been capital of Santa Province. Centre of new iron and steel industries.

CHIPATA, town, Zambia. Formerly Fort Johnson.

CHIRICK, Uzbekistan. New town founded 1963.

CHITTARANJAN, West Bengal, India. New town on R. Barakhar.

CHOWILLA LAKE, formed by dam on Murray R., Australia, where States of South Australia, Victoria and New South Wales join. Is 90 miles long.

CHRISTMAS ISLAND, Indian Ocean, Australia. Until 1957 a part of the then colony of Singapore.

CHURCHILL, New Zealand. Name given in 1963 to South Auckland.

CHURCHILL, Victoria, Australia. Formerly Hazelwood.

CHURCHILL RIVER, Labrador, Canada. Formerly Hamilton R.

CIEPLICE SLASKIE ZDROJ, Lower Silesia, Poland. Formerly Bad Warmbrunn, Germany.

CIUDAD REAL, town, Mexico. Now San Cristobal.

CIUDAD TRUJILO, capital, Dominican Republic. Formerly Santo Domingo.

CLEAR, Alaska, U.S.A. Site of American ballistic missile early warning station.

COALBROOK, Orange Free State, South Africa. Centre of new coal-mines supplying oil-from-coal plant at Sasolburg.

COLLISTON, village, Angus, Scotland. Now Gowanbank.

CONGO REPUBLIC (Brazzaville), formerly the French colony of Middle Congo. Became independent 1960. Area 129,960 sq. miles. Pop.: 864,000. Cap.: Brazzaville.

CONGOLESE REPUBLIC (Kinshasa) or Democratic Republic of the Congo, formerly Belgian Congo. Became independent 1960. In 1966 twenty-one provinces were divided into eight (Central Congo; Bandundu; Equateur; Orientale; Kivi; Katanga; East Kasai; West Kasai). Area: 905,582 sq. miles. Pop.: 15,627,000. Cap.: Kinshasa. Chief industry: copper-mining.

COQUIHATVILLE, Congolese Republic. Now Mbandaka.

CORAL SEA ISLAND TERRITORY, new Australian territory created 1969. Consists of scattered islands east of Queensland beyond Barrier Reef.

CORBY, Northants., England. New town founded 1950. Pop.: 48,000.

CORFU, Greek island. Now Kerkya.

CORONATION HILL, Northern Territory, Australia. Site of big uranium deposits discovered the day of the Queen's Coronation.

CRAWLEY, Sussex, England. New town founded 1947; 9 miles from Reigate. Pop.: 67,400.

CRESTMONT, S. Eagles Mere, Pennsylvania, U.S.A. New town.

CUMBERNAULD, Dunbarton, Scotland. New town near Glasgow. Founded 1955. Pop.: 27,000.

CWMBRAN, Mon., Wales. New town founded 1949, 5 miles N. of Newport. Pop.: 44,100.

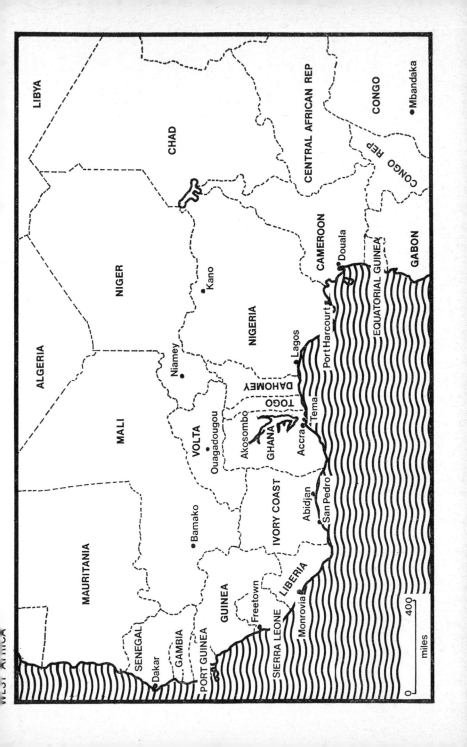

D

DADNA and NAGAR HARELI, Indian Territory formed in 1961 from former Portuguese territory.

DAHOMEY, republic, west African coast. Formerly a colony in French West Africa. Became independent in 1906. Area: 47,000 sq. miles. Pop.: 2,508,000. Cap.: Porto Novo, but chief town and port, Cotonou. Chief industry: palm products.

DAIREN, seaport, S. Liaoning, China. Now Talien.

DAMODAR VALLEY PROJECT, India. Begun in 1947 with hydro-electric power supplying new industries in Tilaiya, Konar, Maithon and Panchet Hill.

DAMPIER, Western Australia. New iron-ore port at mouth of Fitzroy R.

DANUBE–TISA Canal, Vojvodina, Yugoslavia, New waterway. Completed 1970.

DANZIG, Baltic seaport. Now Gdansk, Poland.

DARKHAN, Mongolia. New industrial town on R. Hara.

DEDZA, Malawi. New town built 1966.

DELTA PROJECT, Netherlands, provides for closure by means of massive dams of four broad, deep inlets between the islands of the Rhine-Maas delta (Zeeland).

DENEYSVILLE, Orange Free State, South Africa. New holiday resort on Vaaldam Lake.

DEVON, Alberta, Canada. New town developed after discovery of oil at Leduc in 1947.

DHEKELIA, British sovereign area, Cyprus.

DIEFENBAKER LAKE, Canada, about 50 miles S.W. of Saskatoon. Created by building of Outlook Dam, now Gardiner Dam on South Saskatchewan R. Lake is 100 miles long.

DIMITROVGRAD, S.E. Bulgaria. New industrial town founded 1947.

DIMITROVO, Bulgaria. Formerly Pernik. Old name restored about 1968.

DIMONA, New town, Israel. S. of Dead Sea.

DJAJPURA, capital West Irian, Indonesia. Formerly Kotabaru. Then for brief period Sukarnarpura.

18

DJAKARTA, capital Indonesia, on island of Java. Formerly Batavia. Pop.: nearly 3 millions.

DNEPRORUDNY, South Ukraine, Soviet Union. New town on shores of Kakhovka Sea, an artificial lake, created by dam on R. Dnieper.

DOBRICH, town, Bulgaria. Now Tolbukhin.

DOKUCHAVESK, Donets Basin, Soviet Union. New mining town near Veliky Forest. Founded 1954.

DONETSK, Ukraine, Soviet Union. Formerly Stalino.

DONZÈRE-MONDRAGON, Provence, France. Site of great barrage on R. Rhône, completed 1952.

DUNAUJVÁROS, (Danube New Town), Hungary. Founded 1950 as Stalinvaros. Renamed 1962.

DUSHANBE, town and cap., Tadzhik, Soviet Union. Formerly Stalinabad.

DUSHAVA, West Ukraine, Soviet Union. New town built after Second World War to serve rich natural-gas area.

DUSZNIKI ZDROJ, town, Lower Silesia, Poland. Formerly Bad Reinerz.

DUTCH NEW GUINEA, in W. of island. Now West Irian, Indonesia.

DZHALIL, Soviet Union. New town near new oilfield, 30 miles N.E. of Almetyevsk.

DZIERZONIOUW, town, Lower Silesia, Poland. Formerly Reichenbach, Germany.

E

EAST KILBRIDE, North Lanark, Scotland. New town 7 miles S.E. of Glasgow. Founded 1947. Pop.: 62,584.

EAST PAKISTAN, one of two areas forming Commonwealth Republic of Pakistan. It comprises eastern part of former Bengal Province plus certain additional areas. Area: 55,126 sq. miles. Pop.: 50,840,235. Chief city: Dacca.

EASTERN FLEVOLAND. New province, Netherlands in the Yssel Lake, recovered from water. Brought into use 1965. Covers 136,000 acres. Chief town Lelystad.

EDITH RONNE LAND, Antarctica. In 1967 changed to Ronne Land.

EGER (EILAN), Germany. Now Ilawa, Poland.

ELAT, Israel. New port on Red Sea, near site of ancient port.

ELBLAG, North Poland. Shipbuilding town. Formerly Elbring, East Prussia, Germany.

ELBRING, East Prussia, Germany. Now Elblag, Poland.

ELEKTRANAI, Lithuania, Soviet Union. New town near Vievis at site of thermal power station.

ELIZABETH, South Australia. New town named after the Queen, 17 miles N. of Adelaide.

ELIZABETHVILLE, Congo. Now Lubumbashi.

EL KHARGA, Libyan Desert, United Arab Republic. Capital of New Valley.

EL RAO, Bolivar State, Venezuela. New iron-ore-mining town. New rail line from here to Palma, Orinoco R. Completed 1949.

ELVERSHAGEN, town, Germany. Now Lagiewniki, Upper Silesia, Poland.

ENNEPETAL, North Rhine-Westphalia, Germany. New town on R. Ennape created in 1949 when Milap and Voerde were merged.

EQUATORIAL GUINEA, new republic, West Africa, established in 1968 from former Spanish Guinea. Is divided into two provinces: Rio Muni (Cap.: Bata) and Fernando Po (Cap.: Santa Isabel). Area: 10,800 sq. miles. Pop.: 214,000.

ERITREA, North-east Africa, a province of Ethiopia. Formerly an Italian colony. Incorporated in Ethiopia in 1952. Area: 45,754 sq. miles. Pop.: 1 million. Cap.: Asmara.

EUCUMBENE LAKE, Australia. Created by building largest dam in Snowy R. scheme.

EUROPORT, Netherlands. New port near Rotterdam.

EVANDER, Transvaal, South Africa. New town, 60 miles N. E. of Johannesburg. Established 1960.

EXMOUTH, Western Australia. New town inaugurated 1967.

F

FARIDABAD, town, Punjab, India, S.E. of Delhi.

F'DERIK, port, Mauretania. Formerly Port Gouraud.

FEDERATION OF RHODESIA AND NYASALAND was set up in 1953 to

ANTARCTICA

ANTARCTIC

British Antarctic Territory

Haley Bay Base
Shackleton Base
Ronne Land
South Pole

Mawson

Vostok

Scott Base

Byrd Land

0   600
miles

unite Southern and Northern Rhodesia and Nyasaland. It broke up in 1963 when Northern Rhodesia (Zambia) and Nyasaland (Malawi) were granted independence. Southern Rhodesia in 1965 unconstitutionally declared unilateral independence, and in 1969 voted in favour of a republic.

FERNANDO DE NORONHA, Brazil. New federal territory.

FIUME, Italy. Now Rijeka-Susak, Yugoslavia.

FLEVOSTED, Netherlands. New administrative centre for S.E. Polder.

FLORA, Norway. New city 85 miles N. of Bergen.

FORT GOURAUD, town, Mauretania; 350 miles inland from Nouadhibou (Port Etienne). Developed after discovery of vast iron-ore deposits.

FORT JOHNSON, now Chipata, Zambia.

FORT ROSEBERRY, Zambia. Now Mansa.

FORT THOMPSON, British Columbia, Canada. Now Kamloops.

FORT TRINQUET, town, Mauretania. Now Bir Moghrein.

FOS-SUR-MER, near Marseilles, France. New port under construction.

FRANKENSTEIN, Germany. Now Zabkowice, Poland.

FRENCH SOMALILAND. Now Afars and Issas.

FRENCH WEST AFRICA. Now divided into following independent States: Dahomey; Ivory Coast; Mauretania; Niger; Guinea; Upper Volta; Mali.

FRIANT-KERN CANAL, south-central California, U.S.A. Extends 153 miles along E. side of San Joaquin Valley.

FRIULI-VENEZIA GUILIA, Italy. New autonomous region created 1963, N.E. Italy. It comprises three provinces—Udine, Goriza and Trieste.

G

GABERONES, new capital of Botswana.

GABOON, republic on Atlantic coast of Africa. Formerly a colony of French Equatorial Africa. Became independent State within French community 1958. Area: 101,400 sq. miles. Pop.: 470,000. Cap.: Libreville.

GAGARIN, town, Smolensk Oblast, Soviet Union, W. of Moscow. Formerly Gzhatsk.

GANDHIDHAN, Gujerat, India. New town near Kandla on Gulf of Kutch.

GANDHINAGAR, India. New city, capital of Gujarat State, on Sabarmati R.

GAZLI, Ubekistan, Soviet Union. New town developed after discovery of natural gas 1955.

GDANSK, Poland. Formerly Danzig. Baltic port. Incorporated in Poland 1945.

GERMANY, Federal Republic of, declared Sovereign State May 1955. Consists of 9 Länder (Schleswig-Holstein; Hamburg; Lower Saxony; Bremen; N. Rhine-Westphalia; Hesse; Rhineland; Palatinate; Baden-Wurtemburg; Bavaria). These previously formed British, American, French zones of occupation. Saar incorporated 1956. Area: 95,962. sq. miles. Pop: 57,785,000. excluding W. Berlin (Pop.: 2,163,000). Cap.: Bonn.

GERMANY, Democratic Republic of, consists of former Länder of Brandenburg; Mecklenburg; Saxony; Saxony-Ahnalt and Thuringia and includes Eastern Berlin. These formerly occupied by Soviet Union. Area: 41,380 sq. miles. Pop.: 15,988,000. Cap.: Eastern Berlin.

GHANA, republic within British Commonwealth, West Africa. Formerly British colony of the Gold Coast. Became independent 1957 and, as result of plebiscite, the U.N. Territory of Trans-Volta-Togoland (administered by Britain) was incorporated. Area: 92,100 sq. miles. Pop.: 8 millions. Cap.: Accra. Chief industries: cocoa and gold.

GHANA LAKE, Sask., Canada. Name given in 1957 to lake 130 miles N.E. of Lac La Ronge.

GIVATAYIM, Israel. New town near Tel Aviv.

GIZYCKO, Olsztyn, Poland. Formerly Lotzen, Germany.

GLATZ, Germany. Now Klodzko, Poland.

GLEIWITZ, Germany. Now Gliwce, Poland.

GLENROTHES, Fife, Scotland. New town. Founded 1948. Pop.: 26,000.

GLIWICE, town, Upper Silesia, Poland. Formerly Gleiwitz, Germany.

GODOLLO, Hungary. New town formed from merging of two districts of Aszod and Godollo.

GOLD COAST, West Africa. Now Ghana.

GOLDSWORTHY, Mt., Western Australia. New iron-ore development.

GORNA DZHUMAYS, Bulgaria. Now Blagoyevgrand.

GORNA ORYAKHOVITSA, North Bulgaria. City formed 1949.

GORNY SHEZHNOGORSK, Soviet Union. New tin-mining town in Siberian Arctic on R. Hantaiki.

GORZOW WIELKOPOLSKI, town, Poland. Formerly Landsberg, Germany.

GOWANBANK, Angus, Scotland. Formerly Colliston, village N. of Arbroath.

GRAND COULEE LAKE, Washington, U.S.A. Formed by building world's longest dam on R. Columbus. Is 151 miles long.

GRANTS TOWN, New Mexico, U.S.A. Developed as important industrial centre since 1956.

GREIFENBERG, Germany. Now Gryfice, Poland.

GRUNBERG, Germany. Now Zielona Gora, Poland.

GRYFICE, town, Poland, near Baltic Sea. Formerly Greifenberg, Germany.

GUANABARA, new Brazilian State in which is now situated Rio de Janeiro. New State was created when Brasilia was inaugurated as capital.

GUAPURA, new territory, Brazil. Now Rondona.

GUINEA, W. coast of Africa. Formerly part of French West Africa. Became independent 1958. Area: 96,865 sq. miles. Pop.: 3,702,000. Cap.: Conakry. Chief industries: alumina and iron ore.

GUYANA, sovereign State within British Commonwealth on N.E. coast of South America. Was formerly British colony of British Guiana. Became independent 1966. Area: 83,000 sq. miles. Pop.: 691,000. Cap.: Georgetown at mouth of Demarara R. Chief industries: sugar, rum and diamonds.

GZHATSK, Soviet Union. Now Gagarin.

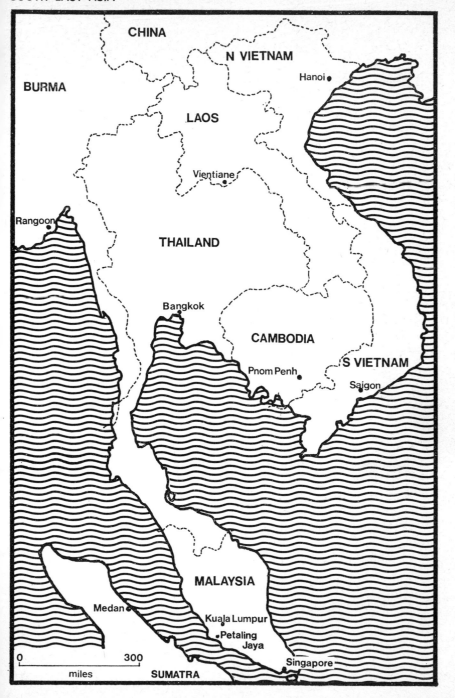

SOUTH EAST ASIA

CHINA

N VIETNAM

BURMA

Hanoi

LAOS

Vientiane

Rangoon

THAILAND

Bangkok

CAMBODIA

S VIETNAM

Pnom Penh

Saigon

MALAYSIA

Medan

Kuala Lumpur

Petaling Jaya

Singapore

0   300

miles

SUMATRA

H

HADERA, new town, Israel, N.W. of Jerusalem.

HALDIA, new satellite port near Calcutta near mouth of R. Hooghli. Completed about 1967.

HALEY BAY BASE, Antarctica. Established 1955 on Caird coast, 200 miles N. of Shackleton.

HAMILTON RIVER, Labrador, Canada. Now Churchill R.

HARIANA, India. New state formed 1966 from part of former state of Punjab. Area: 16,670 sq. miles. Pop.: 7,600,000. Cap.: Chandigarh.

HARINGEY, new London borough, United Kingdom, formed in 1963 by merging former boroughs of Hornsey, Tottenham and Wood Green.

HARLOW, Essex, England. New town founded 1947, 22 miles N.E. of London. Pop.: 75,500.

HASSI-MESSAUD, Algeria. New town near oilfields in Sahara. Has pipe-line to Bejaia.

HATFIELD, Herts., 19 miles N. of London. New town founded 1948. Pop.: 25,300.

HAZELWOOD, Victoria, Australia. Now Churchill.

HEMEL HEMPSTEAD, Herts., England. New town 9 miles N. of Watford. Founded 1947. Pop.: 68,000.

HENNENMAN, Orange Free State, South Africa. New gold-mining town developed since 1950.

HER ZLIYYA, Israel. New town on Mediterranean coast, N. of Tel Aviv.

HIMACHAL PRADESH, new Indian territory created 1948. Area: 10,879 sq. miles. Pop.: 1,351,144. Cap.: Simla.

HINDENBURG, Germany. Now Zabrze, Poland.

HIRAKUD LAKE, Orissa, India. Formed by building dam across Mahanadi R., creating lake of nearly 400,000 acres.

HIRFANLI LAKE, Turkey; is being created by dam on R. Kizlirmak, 90 miles S.E. of Ankara.

HIRSCHBERG, Germany. Now Jelenia Gora, Poland.

HOLON, new town, Israel. S. of Tel Aviv.

HOT SPRINGS, New Mexico, U.S.A. Now Truth and Consequences.

I

ILAWA, town, Olsztyn, Poland. Formerly Eilan, Germany.

ILO, Peru, new port at mouth of Moquegua R.

INDO-CHINA, South-East Asia. Former French dependency. Now divided between the independent States of Vietnam, Cambodia and Laos.

INDONESIA, republic South-East Asia. Formerly Dutch East Indies. Comprises many islands, of which the most important are: Java, Sumatra, Sulawesi, part of Borneo, Bali and West Irian. Area: 735,000 sq. miles. Pop.: 107,000,000. Cap.: Djakarta on Java.

INUVIK, N.W. Territory, Canada. New Eskimo town.

IRVINE, Ayrshire, Scotland. New town adjoining Royal Burgh. Declared new town 1966. Pop.: 36,360.

ISA TOWN, Bahrein. New town 4 miles from Manamah.

ISLAMABAD, Pakistan. New capital under construction, near Rawlpindi, below Himalayas.

ISRAEL, republic on western edge of Asia. Established 1948 and comprising larger part of Palestine, which was formerly a U.N. Trust Territory administered by Britain. Area: 7,992 sq. miles. Pop.: 2,673,000. Chief cities: Jerusalem, Tel Aviv–Yafo. Since 1967 some areas of Jordan occupied and administered by Israel. Chief industries: citrus fruits and by-products.

ISIRO, town N.E. of Congolese Republic. Formerly Paulis.

IVANO-FRANKOVSK, town, Ukraine, Soviet Union. Formerly Stanislav.

IVORY COAST, republic of West Africa. Formerly part of French West Africa. Area: 189,029 sq. miles. Pop.: 4,100,000. Cap.: Abidjan. Chief industries: diamonds and manganese.

IZMAIL, Soviet Union. Port on Danube Estuary, Ukraine. Formerly Roumania.

J

JACOBSTADT, Finland. Now Yekabpils, Kurland, Soviet Union.

JADOTVILLE, Congo. Now Laikasi.

JAWARHARLAL NEHRU CANAL, India. World's largest irrigation canal.

JELENIA GORA, town, Lower Silesia, Poland. Formerly Herschberg, Germany.

JESSELTON, seaport, Sabah, Malaysia. Now Kota Kinabalu.

JOHAANISBURG, Germany. Now Pisz, Poland.

JORDAN, kingdom, W. Asia. Formerly Transjordan and a U.N. International Trust Territory administered by Britain. With establishment of State of Israel part of Palestine, W. of river, was added and new name taken. Area: 34,750 sq. miles. Pop.: 2,071. Cap.: Amman. Chief industry: phosphate.

JURONG, Singapore. New industrial town planned for half million people.

K

KABUE, Zambia. Manufacturing and mining town. Formerly Broken Hill.

KANONKA SEA, Soviet Union. Created by dam on R. Dnieper.

KALEMIE, town, Congolese Republic, on W. Shore of Lake Tanganyika. Formerly Albertville.

KALIMANTAN, Indonesia. Formerly Dutch Borneo. Area: 208,286 sq. miles. Pop.: 4,101,475.

KALININGRAD, Soviet Union, shipbuilding town on R. Pressel. Formerly Königsberg, Germany.

KALYANI, West Bengal, India. New town.

KAMA SEA, Soviet Union. Created by building dam where R. Kama joins the Volga. Stretches for 155 miles.

KAMBALDA, Western Australia. Centre of new nickel discovery and development.

KAMLOOPS, British Columbia, Canada. Formerly Fort Thompson.

KANDLA, Gujarat, India. New port on Gulf of Kutch.

KANPUT, Uttar Pradesh, India. Manufacturing centre. Formerly Cawnpore.

KARA-KUM CANAL, Turkmenia, Soviet Union. 560 miles long. Completed 1962.

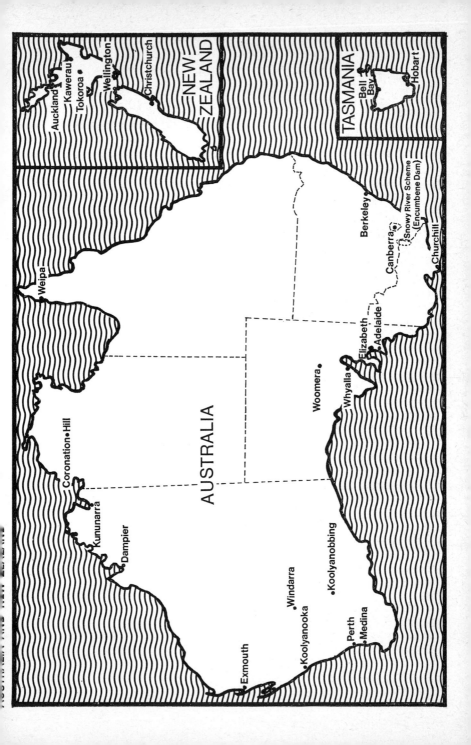

KAREN STATE, Burma. Now Kawthoole.

KARIBA LAKE, between Rhodesia and Zambia. Formed by building dam on R. Zambesi. Stretches for 175 miles. Completed 1960.

KARL-MARX-STADT, East Germany, manufacturing town. Formerly Chemnitz. Chief town of region of same name.

KARMI'EL, Galilee, Israel. New town between Acre and Safad. Inaugurated 1964.

KASHM-EL-GURBA, Sudan. New town replacing Wadi Halfa submerged by inundation of Aswan Dam.

KAWERAU, New Zealand. New town on Bay of Plenty, developed around new forest industries.

KAWTHOOLE STATE, Burma. Formerly Karen State. Area: 11,731 sq. miles.

KAZINCBARCIKA, N.E. Hungary, on Sajs R. Industrial town founded 1951.

KEFAR SAVA, Israel. New town N. of Tel Aviv.

KERALA, Indian State constituted 1956. Consists of most of territory of Travancore-Cohin and Malabar District of Madras. Area: 15,002 sq. miles. Pop.: 16,903,715. Cap.: Trivandrum.

KERKYA, Greek island. Formerly Corfu.

KESZTHELY, Hungary. New holiday resort on Lake Balaton.

KHULNA, East Pakistan, on R. Bhairab. New industrial centre serving port of Chalna.

KINSHASA, capital of Congolese Republic. Formely Leopoldville. Pop.: over 1 million.

KISANGANI, Congolese Republic. Town on R. Congo. Formerly Stanleyville.

KITAKYUSHU, Japan. City created 1963 by merging towns of Moji, Kokura, Tobata, Yawata and Wakamatsu. Pop.: 1,042,389.

KITIMAT, British Columbia, Canada, at head of Douglas Channel. New port and site of great aluminium works.

KLODZKO, town, Lower Silesia, Poland, on R. Neisse. Formerly Glatz, Germany.

KLUCZBORG, town, Upper Silesia, Poland. Formerly Krensburg, Germany.

KNOB LAKE, town, Labrador, Canada. Now Schefferville.

KOLAROVGRAD, Bulgaria. Now Shumen.

KOLBERG, Germany. Now Kolobrzeg, Poland.

KOLOBRZEG, seaport and holiday resort, W. Pomerania, Poland. Formerly Kolberg, Germany.

KOMLO, South Hungary. New manufacturing and mining town. N. of Pecs.

KÖNIGSBERG, East Prussia, Germany. Now Kaliningrad, Soviet Union.

KOOLYANOBBING, Western Australia, new iron-ore development.

KOOLYANOOKA, Western Australia. Near Geraldtown; centre of new iron-ore development.

KOREA, republic, Far East. Was under Japanese rule from 1910 to 1945 and then occupied by American troops in S. and by Soviet troops in N., the dividing line being 38th parallel. After troops were withdrawn two zones remained separate. South Korea: Area: 38,452 sq. miles. Pop.: 28,155,000. Cap.: Seoul. North Korea: 46,814 sq. miles. Pop.: 11,11,000. Cap.: Pyongyang.

KORSAKOV, town, Sakhalin, Soviet Union. Formerly Japan.

KOSLIN, Germany. Now Koszalin, Poland.

KOSSU LAKE, Ivory Coast. Created by dam on Bandama R.

KOSZALIN, town, near Baltic Sea, Poland. Formerly Koslin, Germany.

KOTABARU, West Irian, Indonesia. Now Djajapura.

KOTAKINABALU, seaport, Sabah, Malaysia. Formerly Jesselton.

KOZHIKODE, formerly Calicut, India. Capital of Laccadive, Mincoy and Amindivi Islands off W. coast which form Indian territory.

KRALJEVO, Serbia, Yugoslavia. Now Svetoyarevo.

KRENSBURG, Germany. Now Kluczborg, Poland.

KUDOWA ZDROJ, town, Lower Silesia. Formerly Bad Kudowa, Germany.

KUIBYSHEV SEA, Soviet Union. Created by dam on Middle Volga 30 miles N.W. of Kuibyshev. Completed 1955.

KUNICE, town, near Baltic Sea. Formerly, Kunitz, Germany.

KUNITZ, Germany. Now Kunice, Poland.

KUNUNURRA, Western Australia. New town near Ord R.

KURILE ISLANDS, Pacific Ocean, Soviet Union. Area: 6,160 sq. miles. Pop.: 30,000. Formerly Japan.

L

LACQ, Aquitaine, France. New oil centre.

LADEK, town, Lower Silesia, Poland. Formerly Landau, Germany.

LADEK ZDROJ, town, Lower Silesia, Poland. Formerly Bad Landeck, Germany.

LAGIEWNIKI, town, Upper Silesia, Poland. Formerly Elvershagen, Germany.

LAIKAISI, town, Congolese Republic. Formerly Jadotville.

LANDAU, Germany. Now Ladek, Poland.

LANDSBERG, Germany. Now Gorzow Welkopolski, Poland.

LAOS, kingdom, South-East Asia, formerly part of French Indo-China. Became fully independent 1954. Area: 90,000 sq. miles. Pop.: 2,700,000. Cap.: Vientiane.

LEDUC, central Alberta, Canada, 20 miles S. of Edmonton. Centre of vast new oil wells.

LELYSTAD, Netherlands, built as administrative centre for Eastern Flevoland.

LESOTHO, southern Africa and an enclave within Republic of South Africa, is a kingdom within British Commonwealth. Area: 11,716 sq. miles. Pop.: 1 million. Cap.: Maseru. Formerly British Protectorate of Basutoland.

LIBERTY ISLAND, New York harbour, U.S.A. Formerly Bedloe's Island. Renamed 1956 after Statue of Liberty, which stands on it.

LIBYA, republic, North Africa. Formerly Italian colony. After war administered by Britain and France. Became independent 1951. Area: 679,400 sq. miles. Pop.: 1,195,000. Cap.: Beira (under construction). Chief cities and former capitals: Tripoli and Benghazi.

LIVINGSTONE, West Lothian, Scotland. New town founded 1962. Pop.: 8,180.

LOD, town, Israel, S.E. of Tel Aviv. Formerly Lydda.

LONDON BOROUGHS: (Separate entries for the new names of BRENT, CAMDEN, HARINGEY, NEWHAM, WALTHAM FOREST)

City of Westminster, includes former boroughs of Paddington and St. Marylebone.

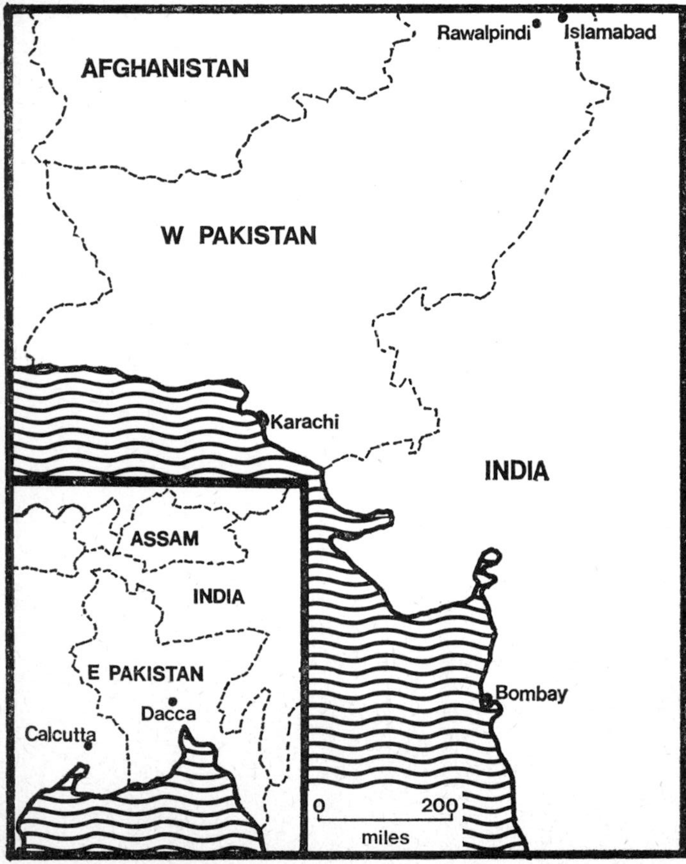
AFGHANISTAN
Rawalpindi
Islamabad
W PAKISTAN
Karachi
INDIA
Bombay
0
200
miles
ASSAM
INDIA
E PAKISTAN
Dacca
Calcutta

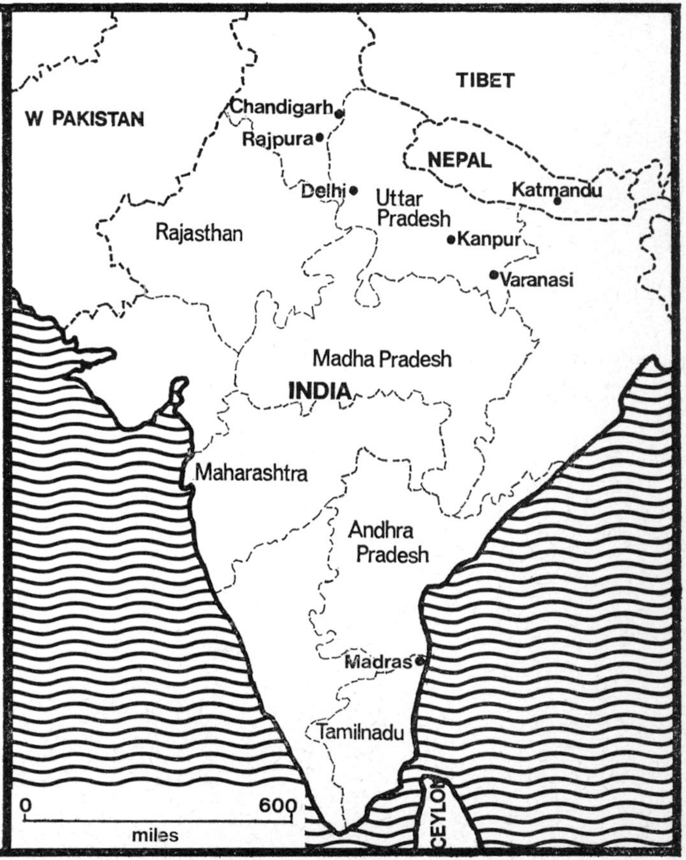
TIBET
W PAKISTAN
Chandigarh
Rajpura
NEPAL
Katmandu
Delhi
Uttar
Pradesh
Kanpur
Varanasi
Rajasthan
Madha Pradesh
INDIA
Maharashtra
Andhra
Pradesh
Madras
Tamilnadu
CEYLON
0
600
miles

Barking, includes most of former borough of Dagenham.

Barnet, includes former borough of Hendon.

Bexley, includes Chislehurst, most of Sidcup, Crayford and Erith.

Brent, new name to describe former boroughs of Willesden and Wembley.

Bromley, includes Beckenham, parts of Chislehurst, Sidcup, and Orpington and Sidcup.

Camden, new name for former boroughs of Hampstead, Holborn and St. Pancras.

Ealing, includes former boroughs of Acton and Southall.

Enfield, includes former boroughs of Edmonton and Southgate.

Greenwich, includes most of Woolwich.

Hackney, includes former boroughs of Shoreditch and Stoke Newington.

Hammersmith, includes former borough of Fulham.

Haringey, new name taken for former boroughs of Hornsey, Tottenham and Wood Green.

Harrow.

Havering, including Hornchurch and Romford.

Hillingdon, including Hayes, Harlington, Ruislip, Northwood and Yiewsley.

Hounslow, includes Brentford, Chiswick, Heston and Isleworth, Feltham and Hounslow.

Islington, including Finsbury.

Kensington and Chelsea, Royal borough.

Kingston-on-Thames, Royal Borough, includes Malden, Coombe and Surbiton.

Lambeth, including part of former borough of Wandsworth with Streatham and Clapham.

Lewisham, including former borough of Deptford.

Merton, including former boroughs of Mitcham, Wimbledon, Merton and Morden.

Newham, new name taken by former boroughs of East and West Ham and parts of Barking and Woolwich.

Redbridge, includes former boroughs of Ilford, Wanstead and Woodford, and parts of Chigwell and Dagenham.

Richmond, including former boroughs of Barnes and Twickenham.

Southwark, includes Bermondsey and Camberwell.

Sutton, including former boroughs of Beddington and Wallington, Sutton and Cheam, and Carshalton.

Tower Hamlets, name for former boroughs of Bethnal Green, Stepney and Poplar.

Waltham Forest, new name assumed by former boroughs of Chingford, Leyton and Walthamstow.

Wandsworth, includes former borough of Battersea.

LOTZEN, Germany. Now Gzycho, Olsztyn, Poland.

LUBIN, town, Lower Silesia, Poland. Formerly Lebbin, Germany.

LUBUMBASHI, Katanga, Congolese Republic. Copper-mining centre. Formerly Elizabethville.

LUGANSK, Ukraine, Soviet Union. Now Voroshilovgrad.

LUSAVAN, town, Armenia, Soviet Union. Now Charentsavan.

LUTA, new municipality, South Liaoning province, China. Established 1952 to combine Port Arthur and Talien.

LUTSK and REVNC, Soviet Union. New province near frontier with Poland. Formerly Volhyn Region. Area: 13,750 sq. miles.

LYDDA, town, Israel. Now Lod.

LYTTELTON, Transvaal, South Africa. Now Verwoerdburg.

M

MADAN, Bulgaria. New industrial and mining town.

MADHYA PRADESH, Indian State formed 1956. Composed of former States of Bhopal, Vindhya Pradesh and Madhya Bharat and certain other districts. Area: 171,210 sq. miles. Pop.: 32,372,408. Cap.: Bhopal.

MADINT-AL-SHAAB, Southern Yemen. Formerly Al Itihad.

MAHARASTHRA, Indian State. Created 1960 when the former state of Bombay was divided into Gujarat and Maharasthra. Area: 118,717 sq. miles. Pop.: 39,563,718. Cap.: Greater Bombay.

MALAGASY REPUBLIC, independent State within French Community on large island in Indian Ocean. Formerly French Protectorate of

Madagascar. Became independent 1960. Area: 227,800 sq. miles. Pop.: 6,180,000. Cap.: Tanarive. Chief industries: graphite and mica.

MALAWI, southern Africa. Republic within British Commonwealth. Formerly British Protcctorate of Nyasaland. Became independent in 1963 when Federation of Rhodesia and Nyasaland broke up. Area: 45,411 sq. miles. Pop.: 4,042,412. Cap.: Zomba, pending construction of new capital near Lilongwe. Chief industries: tea and tobacco.

MALAWI, LAKE, southern Africa. Formerly Lake Nyasa.

MALAYSIA, an independent kingdom in South-East Asia, within the British Commonwealth. Created in 1963 when the Federation of Malaya was enlarged by the accession of Singapore (who withdrew in 1966), Sabah and Sarawak, taking name of Malaysia. Area: 128,478 sq. miles. Pop.: 9,880,134. Cap.: Kuala Lumpur. Chief industries: rubber and tin.

MALI, republic central Africa. Formerly French colony of Sudan. Area: 460,200 sq. miles. Pop.: 4,100,000. Cap.: Bamako.

MANGLA LAKE, Pakistan. Formed by building dam on Jhelum R.

MANSA, town, Zambia. Formerly Fort Rosebery.

MANSINI, Swaziland. Formerly Bremersdorf.

MARIUPOL, Ukraine, Soviet Union. Now Zhadanov.

MARKENWAARD, Netherlands. New polder to be formed N.E. of Amsterdam.

MARSA-EL-BREGA, Libya. New port on Gulf of Sirta. Has oil pipe-line from Zelten.

MARIE BYRD LAND, Antarctica. Now Byrd Land.

MARY KATHLEEN, Queensland, Australia. New town near uranium field.

MASERU, new capital of Lesotho.

MATARINI, S. Peru, Islay Province. Modern port 7 miles from Mollendo.

MAURETANIA, North-west Africa, republic and Member of French Community. Became independent 1960. Formerly part of French West Africa. Area: 419,000 sq. miles. Pop.: 900,000. Cap.: Nouakchott.

THE EAST INDIES

MAWSON, MacRobertson Land, Antarctica. First permanent Australian station on continent established 1954.

MBALA, town, Zambia. Formerly Abercorn.

MBANDAKA, Congolese Republic, capital Equateur province. Formerly Coquilhatville.

MBUJI-MAYI. Congolese Republic, capital of East Kasai Province. Formerly Port Francqui.

MEDINA, Western Australia. New town on Cockburn Sound.

METARIPE, State of Bahla, Brazil. New town that developed around oil refinery.

MEZHDURECHENSK, W. Siberia, Soviet Union on R. Tom. New coal-mining town.

MIDDLE CONGO, French colony of, now Congo Republic (Brazzaville).

MIEDZYZDROJE, town, near Baltic. Formerly Misdroy, Germany.

MIELNO, town, Poland. Formerly Mollen, Germany.

MILTON KEYNES, Bucks, England. Site of new city covering 3 sq. miles and embracing Bletchley, Wolverton and Stony Stratford.

MINA-AL-AHMADI, Kuwait. New oil port 5 miles from Ahmadi.

MINA HASSAN TANI, town, Morocco. Formerly Port Lyautey.

MIRNY, Antarctica. Soviet Base. Is along 90° of longitude.

MISDROY, town, Germany. Now Miedzyzdroje, Poland.

MITTEL SCHREIBERHAN, Germany. Now Szklarska Poreba, Poland.

MLADA BOLESLAW, Bohemia, Czechoslovakia. Formerly Jungbunzlaw.

MOJI, Japan, town. Now part of city of Kitakyushu.

MOLE HILL, W. Virginia, U.S.A. Now Mountain.

MOLLEN, town, Germany. Now Mielno, Poland.

MOONIE, Queensland, Australia, not far from Brisbane. New town near site of Australia's chief oilfields.

MOROCCO, kingdom, North-west Africa. Larger part was former French protectorate; small area, Spanish protectorate and former international Zone of Tangier. These formed in 1956 independent State. Area: 171,000 sq. miles. Pop.: 11,626. Cap.: Rabat.

MOUNEAUX-LA-NEUVE, Aquitaine, France. New town developed as result of discovery of natural gas at Lacq.

MOUNTAIN, West Virginia, U.S.A., town. Formerly Mole Hill.

MOUNT GOLDSWORTHY, Western Australia. New iron-ore centre.

MOUNT TOM PRICE, Western Australia. New town under construction for new iron-ore development.

MOUNT WHALEBACK, Western Australia. New iron-ore centre.

MTWARA, Tanzania, new port built in 1948 near Mikidani.

N

NAGALAND, India. New State near Burma border, inaugurated 1963 out of parts of Assam. Area: 6,366 sq. miles. Pop.: 369,000. Cap.: Kohima.

NAHARIYYA, Israel. New coastal town N. of Haifa.

NAKEL, Germany, town. Now Naklo, Poland.

NAKHODKA, Soviet Union. New port on Sea of Japan. 45 miles E. of Vladivostok. Created 1950. Pop.: 63,000.

NAKLO, town, Poland. 50 miles from Baltic coast. Formerly Nakel, Germany.

NAMIBIA, formerly South-west Africa. International Trust Territory under United Nations, which South Africa has incorporated into the Republic. Area: 318,161 sq. miles. Pop.: 525,064. Cap.: Windhoek.

NANGAL, new town, India, near Bhakra-Nangal dam.

NASSER CITY, United Arab Republic. Built at Kom Ombare to settle 50,000 Nubians displaced by formation of Lake Nasser.

NASSER LAKE, United Arab Republic, created by the building of the new Aswan Dam.

NAURU, island republic and world's smallest independent State. Became independent in 1968. Formerly International Trust Territory administered by Australia. Area: $8\frac{1}{4}$ sq. miles. Pop.: 6,956. Cap.: Nauru.

NEWFOUNDLAND, North America. Until 1949 it, with its dependency Labrador, was a British Dominion. It then voted to become Canada's 10th Province. Area: 156,185 sq. miles. Pop.: 500,000. Cap.: St. John's.

NEWHAM, new London borough. Comprises former County boroughs of East and West Ham; part of Barking and Woolwich N. of Thames. Took new name in 1965.

NEWMAN, Mount, Western Australia. Centre of iron-ore development. New town under construction.

NEW MIRPUR, Pakistan. New town near Mangla dam.

NEW SAULT, Canada. New town on St. Lawrence Seaway, near the Eisenhower Lock.

NEWTON, Montgomery, Wales. Declared new town 1967.

NEW VALLEY, United Arab Republic. Extends 75 miles from Aswan to the Qattara Depression. Land has been reclaimed from desert by water from underground river.

NHULUNBY, new town, Cove Peninsula, Northern Territory, Australia. Built for bauxite development.

NIGER, republic in West central Africa. Formerly part of French West Africa. Became independent 1960. Area: 484,000 sq. miles. Pop.: 4,033,500. Cap.: Niamey. Chief industries: groundnuts and livestock.

NILOKHERI, Punjab, India. New town.

NORTH BORNEO, now Sabah, Malaysia.

NORTHAMPTON, although designated a new town in 1968, it is in fact to be a massive expansion of the County borough of that name.

NORTHERN RHODESIA, central Africa. Now Zambia.

NOUADHIBOU, Mauretania. Formerly Port Etienne.

NOUKACHOTT, capital Mauretania. Built when country became independent in 1960.

NOVA GORICA, western Slovenia, Yugoslavia. New town developed after 1947.

NOVA HUTA, Poland. New town near Cracow on R. Vistula. Developed as steel centre in 1949.

NOVAMOSKOVSK, Soviet Union, on R. Don. Formerly Stalinogorsk.

NOVA TROITSK, Orenburg Region, Soviet Union. New town in Urals. Centre of iron and steel works.

NOVAYA KAKHOVKA, Soviet Union, Kherson Region. New town on bank of Danube at beginning of South Ukranian Canal. Founded 1945.

CANADA

GREENLAND

Princess Margaret Range

Queen Elizabeth Islands

Prince Charles Island

Inuvik

ALASKA

Kitimat

Leduc

Atomic City

Ghana Lake

Churchill/R

CANADA

Ungava

Schefferville

Montreal

St Lawrence Seaway

Atikokan

USA

0   600
|————————|
     miles

NOVO-ILIJSK, town, Kazak, Soviet Union. New town near the Kapcagaj power station.

NOVOKUZNETSK, Soviet Union, large industrial town. Formerly Stalinsk.

NOWA TYCHY, Silesia, Poland. New town.

NSANJE, port, Malawi, on Shire R. Formerly Port Herald.

NUKHA, Azerbaijan, Soviet Union. Now Sheki.

NYASALAND, central Africa. Now Malawi.

O

OKHA, port, Sakhalin, Soviet Union. Formerly Japan.

OLECKO, Olsztyn, Poland, town. Formerly Trenburg, Germany.

OLSYTYN, North-west Poland, capital of province of same name. Formerly Allenstein, Germany. Town is on R. Alle.

OROSZLANY, Hungary. New mining town developed from village of same name.

ORTELSBURG, Germany. Now Szczytno, Poland.

OZD, Hungary. New town near Miskolcz, centred round steel works.

P

PAKISTAN, Islamic Republic of, came into being in 1956, having been since 1947 a British Dominion when it adopted officially the name of Pakistan. It is a member of the British Commonwealth. Pakistan consists of two geographical units, East Pakistan and West Pakistan. Area: 365,529 sq. miles. Pop.: 102,876. Cap.: Islamabad, near Rawalpindi. Chief industries: jute and cotton products.

PALESTINE, or Holy Land. Formerly under League of Nations mandate, administered by United Kingdom. Now divided between Israel and Jordan.

PANJIM, India, capital of Goa, Daman and Diu. Formerly Nova Goa and a Portuguese enclave until 1961.

PARADEEP, Orissa, India. New port being developed on lake formed by Hirakud dam across Mahanadi R.

PARENTIS, France. New lignite mines centre 40 miles S.W. of Bordeaux.

PAULIS, Congolese Republic. Now Isiro.

PECHENGA, Soviet Union, narrow strip 135 miles long from North Finland to near Varanger Fjord, Norway. Area: 3,860 sq. miles. Pop.: 12,000. Cap.: port of same name. Was formerly Petsamo, Finland.

PERM, Soviet Union, on R. Kama, N.W. of Sverdlovsk. Formerly Molotov.

PETAH TIGUA, Israel. New town near Tel Aviv.

PETALING JAYA, Selangar, Malaysia. New town near Kuala Lumpur.

PETERBOROUGH, Hunts. Although designated a new town in 1967, it will in fact be an extension of the existing municipal borough.

PETERLEE, new town, Durham, England. Named in 1948 after miner's leader, when construction began. Pop.: 21,250.

PETSAMO, Finland. Now Pechenga, Soviet Union.

PHALABORWA, Transvaal, South Africa. Established 1957.

PHOUOKHAO-KHUAI, Laos, mountain resort, about 20 miles N. of Vientiane. Formerly Ritaville.

PIEKARY, town, Lower Silesia, Poland. Formerly Beckern, Germany.

PILA, town, North-west Poland. Formerly Schneidermuhl, Pomerania, Germany.

PILAWA, town, Lower Silesia, Poland. Formerly Beilar, Germany.

PISZ, town, Olsztyn, Poland. Formerly Johaanisburg, Germany.

POLANICA ZDROJ, town, Lower Silesia, Poland. Formerly Alheide, Germany.

POLCZYN ZDROJ, Lower Silesia, Poland. Formerly Bad Polzin, Germany.

POLESIE, district divided between Ukraine and Belorussia, Soviet Union. Cap.: Brest Litovsk. Formerly a Polish department.

POLICE, town, Upper Silesia, Poland. Formerly Politz, Germany.

POLOTSKIY, Belorussia, Soviet Union. New oil town.

PORONAISK, town, Sakhalin, Soviet Union. Formerly Japan.

PORT ARTHUR, S. Liaoning Province, China. Now incorporated with Talien in new municipality of Luta.

PORT ARZEW, Algeria, port and site of natural-gas plant. Opened 1964.

PORT ETIENNE, Mauretania. Now Nouhadhibou.

PORT FRANCQUIN, town, Congolese Republic. Now Mbuji-Mayi.

PORT GOURAUD, Mauretania. Now F'derik.

PORT HERALD, Malawi. Now Nsanje.

PORT LYAUTEY, Morocco. Now Mina Hassan Tani.

PRINCE CHARLES ISLAND, N. of Hudson Bay, Canada. Named after Prince of Wales.

PRINCESS MARGARET RANGE, Canada. On Axel Heiberg.

PUERTO HIERRO, North-east Venezuela, new iron-ore port on Gulf of Paria.

Q

QIRYAT MALAHI, Israel. New town S.W. of Jerusalem.

QIRYAT SHEMONA, Israel. New town N. of Sea of Galilee.

QUEEN ELIZABETH ISLANDS, part of Arctic Archipelago. Named 1954.

QUEZON CITY, Philippines. Being constructed as future capital to replace Manila.

R

RAJASTHAN, Indian State. Came into being between 1948 and 1956 through merging of two former Princely States, together with parts of former States of Bombay and Madhya Bharat. Area: 132,147 sq. miles. Pop.: 20,155,602.

RAJASTHAN CANAL, Rajasthan State, India. One of longest in world. Will be completed about 1975.

RAJPURA, Punjab, India. New town.

RAMLA, town, Israel. Formerly Ramleh.

RANDBURG, Transvaal, South Africa. Town established 1959. Pop: 46,150.

RARGAT GAN, Israel. New town near Tel Aviv.

REDDITCH, Worcs., England. New town founded 1964. Pop.: 36,500.

REHOVOT, Israel. New town S. of Tel Aviv.

REICHENBACH, Germany. Now Dzierzonlow, Poland.

REPELEN-BAERL, Germany. Now Rheinkamp.

CENTRAL AND EASTERN EUROPE

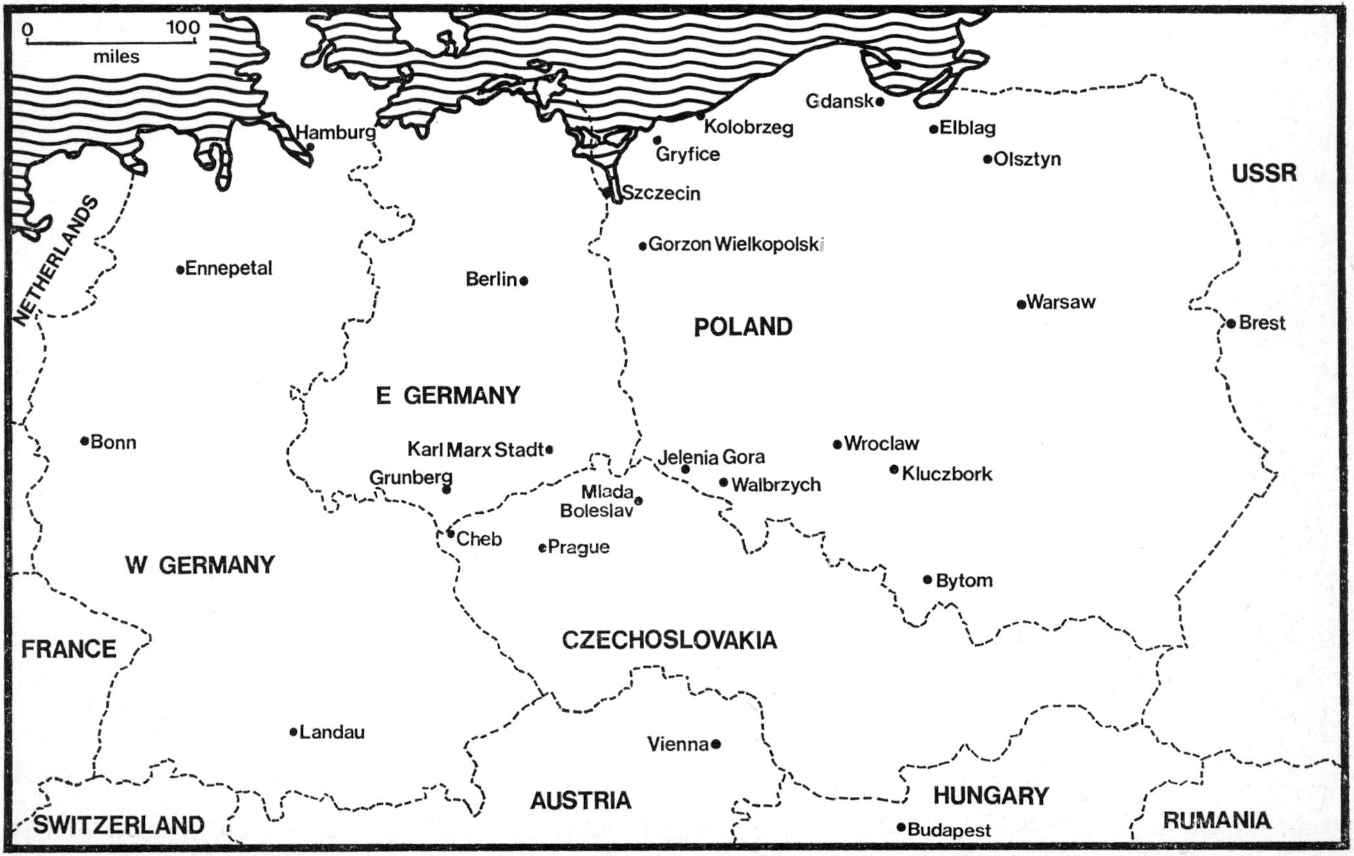

REPUBLIC OF SOUTH AFRICA. Formerly Union of South Africa. Withdrew from British Commonwealth 1961.

RÉUNION, Ile de la, French island in Indian Ocean between Mauritius and Malagassy. Formerly Bourbon.

RHEINKAMP, town, Rhine-Westphalia, Germany. Formerly Repelen-Baerl.

RICHARD'S BAY, South Africa, 100 miles N. of Durban. To be developed as Republic's largest port. New aluminium smelter being built.

RIJEKA-SUSAK, port, Yugoslavia. Formerly Fiume.

RIO BRANCO, Brazil. Now Roraima.

RISHON LE ZION, Israel. New town, S. of Tel Aviv.

ROARING CREEK, British Honduras. Site of new capital.

ROBE RIVER, Western Australia. New iron-ore centre.

ROCKALL, island, North Atlantic Ocean. Annexed by Britain 1955.

RONDONIA, Brazil. New territory. Formerly Guapura.

RONNE LAND, Antarctica. Formerly Edith Ronne Land.

RORAIMA, North Brazil. New territory, bordering Venezuela and Guyana. Formerly Rio Branco.

RUANDA-URUNDI, former U.N. Trust Territory under Belgian administration. Now two independent republics of Burundi and Rwanda.

RUDNYY, Kazak, Soviet Union. New town 30 miles S.W. of Kustanay, iron-ore centre.

RUDOZEM, Bulgaria. New mining town.

RUNCORN, Cheshire, England. New town founded 1964 on S. side of Mersey estuary. Pop.: 31,500.

RUTHENIA, formerly Czechoslovakia. Now Zakarpatskaya (Transcarpathia) Soviet Union.

RUSTAVI, Georgia, Soviet Union. New town 20 miles S.E. of Tibilsi.

RWANDA, independent republic, central Africa. Formerly part of U.N. Trusteeship Territory, administered by Belgium, known as Ruanda-Urundi. Became independent 1962. Area: 10,169 sq. miles. Pop.: 3,018,000. Cap.: Kigali.

RYBINSK, town, Soviet Union. For a short time Shcherbakov.

RYBINSK SEA, Soviet Union. Created by dam on Upper Volga. Eighty miles long and 35 miles wide.

S

SABAH, Malaysia. Formerly North Borneo. Cap.: Kota Kinabalu.

SABAHIYAH, Kuwait. New town under construction between Ahmadi and Fahahil.

SAFAD, town, Israel. Now Zefat, Israel.

SAGAN, Germany. Now Zagan, Poland.

ST. LAWRENCE SEAWAY, Canada–U.S.A. Links Great Lakes with Atlantic Ocean. Opened 1959.

SAKHALIN ISLAND, Soviet Union. Japanese from 1905 to 1945.

SAN CRISTOBAL, town, Mexico. Formerly Ciudad Real.

SANDTON, Transvaal, South Africa. Pop: 55,000.

SAN JUAN BAY, Peru. New port opened 1953.

SAN PEDRO, Ivory Coast. New port being built about 200 miles S.W. of Abidjan.

SANTO DOMINGO, Dominican Republic. Now Ciudad Trujilo.

SASOLBURG, Orange Free State, South Africa. New town, centre of world's largest oil-from-coal plant.

SANTO TOME DE LA GUYANA, new industrial city S.E. of Venezuela, near confluence of Orinoco and Caroni Rivers.

SCHEFFERVILLE, town, Labrador, Canada. Formerly Knob Lake.

SCHWEIDNITZ, Germany. Now Swidnica, Poland.

SCOTT BASE, Antarctica, on McMurdo Sound. Named 1958.

SCUTARI, town, Albania. Now Shkodra.

SCUTARI, Turkey. Now Usküdar.

SENEGAL, West Africa. Independent State within French Community. Formerly part of French West Africa. Area: 77,814 sq. miles. Pop.: 3,580,000. Cap.: Dakar.

SHACKLETON BASE, Antarctica, Vashel Bay. Named 1956.

SHAMALDY-SAY, Kirghiz, Soviet Union. New town on site of hydro-electric power station, near Uch-Kurgar.

SHASTA LAKE, California, U.S.A. Created by dam on Sacramento R. near Redding. Shores stretch for 365 miles.

SHCHERBAKOV, town, Soviet Union. Former name of Rybinsk now restored.

SHEFARAM, town, Israel. Formerly Shafa Amr.

SHEKI, town, Azerbaijan, Soviet Union. Formerly Nukha.

SHENYAN, China, city. Formerly Mukden. Pop.: 2,411,000.

SHKODRA, town, Albania. Formerly Scutari.

SHUMEN, town, Bulgaria, S.E. of Ruse. Formerly Kolarovgrad.

SKELMERSDALE, Lancashire, England. New town. Founded 1961. Pop.: 18,600.

SOMALIA, republic on N.E. horn of Africa. It consists of the former British protectorate of Somaliland and the former Italian International Trust Territory of Somalia. Formed 1960. Area: 246,000 sq. miles. Pop.: 2,580,000. Cap.: Mogadishu.

SOUTH AUCKLAND, New Zealand. Now Churchill.

SOUTH EASTERN FLEVOLAND, Netherlands. Newly reclaimed polder in the Yssel Lake (former Zuyder Zee). Administrative centre: Flevostad.

SOUTH-WEST AFRICA, U.N. International Trust Territory. Now Namibia.

SOUTHERN SAKHALIN, Soviet Union, island, N. of Japan. Formerly Japan.

SOUTHERN YEMEN, People's Republic of, S.W. Arabia. Comprises former British colony of Aden and Protectorate of South Arabia and islands of Perim and Kamara. Became independent 1967. Area: 111,075 sq. miles. Pop.: 1,220,000. Cap.: Aden.

SOWJETSK, Soviet Union on R. Memel. Formerly Tilsit, Germany.

SNOWY RIVER SCHEME, New South Wales and Victoria, Australia. Begun 1950. To be completed 1975. Is providing hydro-electric power and irrigation.

SPANISH GUINEA, West Africa. Now Equatorial Guinea.

SPANISH MOROCCO, was handed over to Morocco in 1956 by Spain when it became independent. Spanish Morocco lay in the North and stretched from the Riff Mountains to the Mediterranean. Area: 11,236 sq. miles. Pop.: 1,982,000. Cap.: Tetuan.

STALIN, Roumania. Now Brasov.

STALIN CANAL, Soviet Union. Now Volga–Baltic Canal.

ISRAEL

LEBANON
Qiryat Shermona
•Nahariyya
Zefat
•Akko
SYRIA
Karmi'el •
Sea of Galilee
•Shefar 'am
Haifa
Tiberias

Zikhron
•Yaagov
•Afula
Bet She'an•

•Hadera

•Netanya

Herzliyya • •Kefar Sava
Ramat Gan •Bene Beraq
Tel Aviv–Yafo • •Petah Tiqwa
•Givatayim
Bat Yam • •Holon
Rishon Le Zion •Lod
•Ramla
•Rehovot
•Ashdod

JORDAN

•Jerusalem
Qiryat •Bet Shemesh
•Malakhi
Ashqelon •
Dead Sea
•Qiryat Gat

ISRAEL

•Arad

•Beersheva

•Dimona

0   24
miles

STALINABAD, town, Soviet Union. Now Dushanbe.

STALINGRAD, Soviet Union. Now Volgograd.

STALINO, town, Bulgaria. Now Varna.

STALINO, town, Ukraine, Soviet Union. Now Donetsk.

STALINOGORSK, Soviet Union. Now Novomoskovsk.

STALINSK, Soviet Union. Now Novokuznetsk.

STANISLAWOW, subdivision, S.W. Ukraine, Soviet Union. Formerly department, Poland.

STANLEYVILLE, Congolese Republic. Now Kisanganu.

STEVENAGE, Herts., England. New town 4 miles S.E. of Hitchin. Founded 1946. Pop.: 62,200.

STETTIN, Germany. Now Szczecin, Poland.

STRNISCE, North-east Slovenia, Yugoslavia. New town centred on aluminium plant.

STUTTHOF, Germany. Now Sztutowo, Poland.

SUI, Baluchistan, Pakistan. Centre of vast reservoir of natural gas.

SUKARNARPURA, West Irian, Indonesia. Now Djajpura.

SULAWESI, Indonesia, island. Formerly Celebes.

SVETOZAREVO, town, Serbia. Yugoslavia. Formerly Kraljevo.

SWIDNICA, town, Lower Silesia, Poland. Formerly Schweidnitz, Germany.

SWIERADOW ZDROJ, town, Lower Silesia, Poland. Formerly Bad Flinsberg, Germany.

SWINEMUNDE, Germany. Now Swinoujscie, Poland.

SWINOUJSCIE, town, Baltic, Poland. Formerly Swinemunde, Germany.

SZARVAS, Hungary. New town developed from village of same name.

SZCZYTNO, town, Olsztyn, Poland. Formerly Ortelsburg, Germany.

SZCZAWNO ZDROJ, town, Lower Silesia, Poland. Formerly Bad Salzbrunn, Germany.

SZCZECIN, seaport, Pomerania, Poland. Formerly Stettin, Germany.

SZKLARSKA POREBA, town, Lower Silesia, Poland. Formerly Mittel Schreiberhau, Germany.

SZTUTOWO, town, Baltic Sea, Poland. Formerly Stutthof, Germany.

SZYALINVAROS, Hungary, town. Now Dunaujaros.

T

TAHIR, or Liberation, United Arab Republic. New province on reclaimed desert between Cairo and Alexandria.

TALIEN, South Liaoning province, China. Seaport: Bay of Korea. Formerly Dairen and now part of enlarged municipality of Luta.

TAMILNADU, India. Formerly Madras State.

TANGANYIKA, mainland area of Tanzania and former U.N. International Trust Territory under British administration. Became independent in 1961.

TANGIER, International Zone of, now an integral part of kingdom of Morocco.

TANZANIA, East Central Africa, republic within British Commonwealth. Composed of former Commonwealth countries of Tanganyika and Zanzibar. Union took place in 1964 when new name assumed. Area: 362,820 sq. miles. Pop.: 12,231,342. Cap.: Dar-es-Salaam. Chief industries: sisal production and diamonds.

TARNOPOL, department of Poland. Now Ternopil, Ukraine, Soviet Union.

TATA, North-west Hungary. New holiday resort on Lake Balaton.

TEL AVIV and JAFFA, Israel. Now Tel Aviv-Yafo.

TELFORD, new town, Shropshire, England. Name given when designated new town in 1968.

TEMA, Ghana. New port, 19 miles E. of Accra; Africa's largest artificial harbour. Opened 1962. Big industrial town alongside has been developed for population of quarter of million.

TERNOPIL, Ukraine, Soviet Union, province with capital city of same name. Formerly Tarnopol, a department of Poland.

THAMESMEAD, new town being constructed on reclaimed Thames marshland, near Woolwich Arsenal and Erith. Area: 1,300 acres. Planned pop.: 80,000.

THAUER, Germany. Now Turow, Poland.

TIKSI BAY, Yakut, Soviet Union. New Arctic seaport.

TILSIT, Germany. Now Sowjetsk, Soviet Union.

TIRUCHIRAPALLI, Tamilnadu, India. Town on R. Cauvery. Formerly Trichinopoly.

TITOGRAD, Yugoslavia. Chief town of Montenegro, built on site of Podgorica.

TOBARAO, Brazil. New port near Victoria.

TOGLIATTI, Soviet Union. Town on River Volga, N.W. of Kuybyshev. Formerly Stavropol.

TOGO, republic of West Africa and former U.N. International Trust Territory under French administration. Became independent 1960. Area: 21,220 sq. miles. Pop.: 1,440,000. Cap.: Lome.

TOKAROA, New Zealand. New town, 136 miles from Auckland, centred round new paper industry.

TOLBUKHIN, town, Bulgaria. Formerly Dobrich.

TOM PRICE, MT., Western Australia. New iron-ore centre.

TRANSCARPATHIA, or Zakarpatskaya, Ukraine, Soviet Union. Formerly Ruthenia, Czechoslovakia.

TRANSJORDAN, name by which the Kingdom of Jordan was known before 1948 when it acquired additional territory.

TRENBURG, Germany. Now Olecko, Poland.

TRIESTE, FREE TERRITORY. Since 1954 divided between Italy and Yugoslavia. City and harbour and Trieste, including Duino to Italy. The towns of Capodistria and Cittanuova to Yugoslavia.

TRUST TERRITORY OF THE PACIFIC ISLANDS. Administered by the United States. Formerly under Japanese mandate. Consists of 96 islands, of which the Marians (except Guam) and the Marshalls are chief. Area: 687 sq. miles. Pop.: 91,448. Cap.: Saipan. Cap.: Mariana islands.

TSCHARNERGUT, Switzerland. New town near Berne, W. of the city.

TUROW, town, Lower Silesia, Poland. Formerly Thauer, Germany.

TUVA, Autonomous Republic of Soviet Union, established 1961. Prior to 1945 it had been a semi-independent State N.W. of Mongolia.

TZEPO, Shantung, China. New city formed by merging Tzechwan, Poshan and Chanchow.

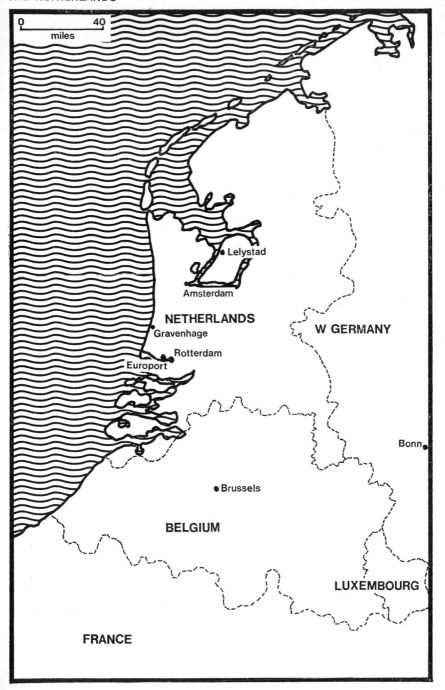

0   40
miles

Lelystad
Amsterdam

NETHERLANDS
Gravenhage
Rotterdam
Europort

W GERMANY

Bonn

Brussels

BELGIUM

LUXEMBOURG

FRANCE

U

UBANGHI SHARI, French colony. Now Central African Republic.

UGLEGORSK, town, Sakhalin, Soviet Union. Formerly Japan.

ULHASNAGAR, Maharastra, India. New city.

UNITED ARAB REPUBLIC, name taken by Egypt in 1958 when a union with Syria was agreed upon. Although this union lasted only three years, Egypt retained the title.

UPPER VOLTA, or Voltaic Republic. West African republic. Formerly part of French West Africa. Area: 100,000 sq. miles. Pop.: 5,504,000. Cap.: Ougadougu.

URANIUM CITY, Saskatchewan, Canada, near Lake Athabasca. Founded. 1951 as centre of uranium mining.

URAVAN, Colorado, U.S.A., centre of uranium and vanadium mining on R. San Miguel.

URUNDI, central Africa. Now Burundi.

USKUDAR, town, Turkey, on Bosphorus. Formerly Scutari.

USUMBURA, Africa. Now Bujumbura.

UTTAR PRADESH, Indian State. Formerly known as United Provinces. Area: 113,654 sq. miles. Pop.: 73,746,401. Cap.: Bareilly.

V

VAAL PARK, Orange Free State, South Africa. New residential town on Vaal River.

VANDERBIJL PARK, Transvaal, South Africa, on Vaal R. Developed after 1946 as centre of big steel works.

VARANASI, city, Uttar Pradesh, India. Formerly Benares.

VARNA, seaport, Bulgaria. Formerly Stalin.

VELIKI BECKEREK, Voivodina, Yugoslavia. Now Zrenjanin.

VERWOERDBURG. Transvaal, town S. of Pretoria. Formerly Lyttelton. Name changed 1967. Pop.: 26,650.

VIETNAM, part of former French Indo-China and comprising Tonking, Annam and Cochin-China. Since 1954 has been divided into two zones. In south, Republic of Vietnam: Area: 66,300 sq. miles.

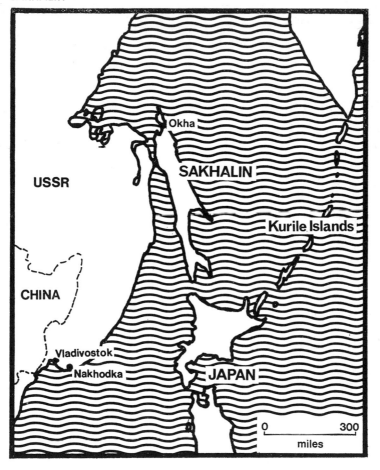

Pop.: 14,000,000. Cap.: Saigon. In north, the Democratic Republic. Area: 63,000 sq. miles. Pop.: 15,903,000. Cap.: Hanoi.
VIRGINIA, Orange Free State, South Africa. New gold-mining town.

55

VOLGA BALTIC WATERWAY, Soviet Union. An inland network of deep water for navigation linking Black Sea and Caspian Sea in S. with Baltic Sea in N.

VOLGOGRAD, city on R. Volga, S. of Saratov. Formerly Stalingrad.

VOLHYN REGION, Soviet Union, near frontier with Poland to which it belonged until 1939. Is now the province of Lutsk and Rovno. Area: 13,750 sq. miles.

VOLTA LAKE, Ghana, one of the largest artificial lakes in world. It covers 3,275 sq. miles and was created by building dam at Akosombo on R. Volta.

VOLTA REDONDA, town, Brazil, near Rio de Janeiro. New iron-ore producing centre.

VOLZHSKY, Soviet Union. New town. 10 miles E. of Volgograd.

VORKUTA, Siberia, Soviet Union. New coal-mining district, 120 miles W. of mouth of R. Ob.

VOROSHILOVGRAD, Ukraine, Soviet Union; industrial centre, Donets Basin. Formerly Lugansk.

VOSTOK, Antarctica. Soviet scientific station 875 miles from coast. S. geomagnetic Pole.

W

WALBRZYCH, town, Lower Silesia, Poland. Formerly Waldenburg, Germany.

WALDENBURG, Germany. Now Walbrzych, Poland.

WASHINGTON, Durham, England. New town founded 1964, 5 miles S.E. of Gateshead. Pop.: 24,300.

WEGORZEWO, town, Olstyn, Poland. Formely Angerburg, Germany.

WEGROW, town, Lower Silesia, Poland. Formerly Bingerau, Germany.

WEIPA, Queensland, Australia, on Cape Tork peninsular. New town and port developed after discovery of bauxite.

WELKOM, Orange Free State, South Africa, centre of largest new gold and uranium deposits in State.

WELWYN GARDEN CITY, Herts., England. New town founded 1948. Pop.: 42,500.

WEST BENGAL, Indian State. Formerly part of Province of Bengal. In 1947 province was divided between India and Pakistan. West Bengal includes former State of Coch Behar, the French settlement of Chandernagore and certain parts of Bihar. Area: 33,829 sq. miles. Pop.: 34,926,270. Chief city: Calcutta.

WEST IRIAN, Indonesia. Formerly Dutch colony of West New Guinea. Incorporated in Indonesia 1963. Area: 115,861 sq. miles. Pop.: 758,396. Cap.: Djajpura.

WHYELLA, South Australia, new steel-producing centre on Spencer Gulf.

WINDARRA, Western Australia, near Leonora. Site of vast new nickel deposits.

WOOMERA, South Australia, 270 miles N.W. of Adelaide. Guided-weapon testing base established 1947.

WROCKLAW, town, Lower Silesia, Poland. Formerly Breslau, Germany.

WUHAN, Hupeh, China. New industrial city formed by merging Hankow, Hanyang and Wuchang. Pop.: 1,427,000.

Y

YANGI-YER, Uzbekistan, Soviet Union. New town founded 1957 as centre for new irrigated cotton lands.

YEKABPILS, town, Kurland, Soviet Union. Formerly Jacobstadt, Finland.

YEVATORIYA, Ukraine, Soviet Union. New port under construction.

YUZHNO, Sakhalinsk, town, Soviet Union at S. end of Sakhalin Island. Formerly Japan.

Z

ZABKOWICE SLASKIE, town, Lower Silesia. Formerly Frankenstein, Germany.

ZABRZE, town, Upper Silesia, Poland. Formerly Hindenburg, Germany.

ZAFAT, town, Israel. Formerly Safad.

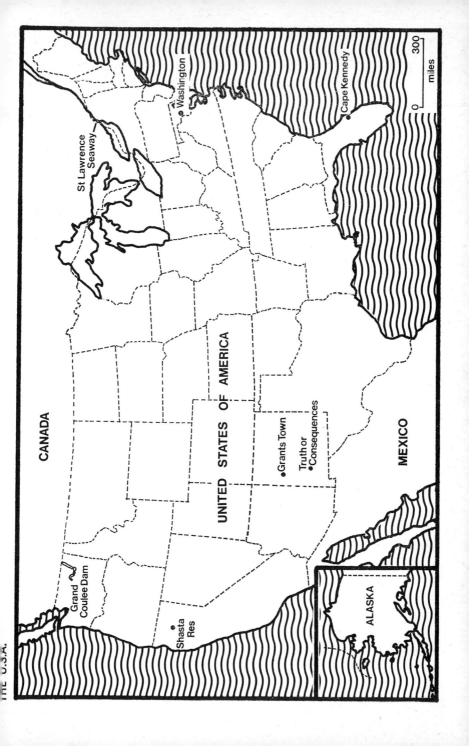

THE U.S.A.

ZAGAN, town, Lower Silesia, Poland. Formerly Sagan, Germany.

ZAKARPATSKAYA (Transcarpathia), Soviet Union. Formerly Ruthenia, Czechoslovakia.

ZAMBIA, central Africa, republic within British Commonwealth. Formerly British Protectorate of Northern Rhodesia and from 1953 to 1963 part of Federation of Rhodesia and Nyasaland. In 1964 Zambia became independent and took new name. Area: 288,130 sq. miles. Pop.: 3,500,000. Cap.: Lusaka. Chief industry: copper mining.

ZELTEN, Fezzan, Libya. Site of vast new oilfields with pipe-line to Marso-al-Brega.

ZHADANOV, seaport, Ukraine, Soviet Union, on Azov Sea. Formerly Mariopul.

ZIELONA GORA, town, Silesia, Poland. Formerly Grunberg, Germany.

ZIKHRON YAAGOV, Israel. New town S. of Haifa.

ZIMBABWE, Rhodesia. Site of ancient ruins and name used by many Africans to describe Rhodesia.

ZRENJANIN, Vojvodina, Yugoslavia on R. Begej. Formerly Veliki Beckerek.

COUNTRIES OF THE WORLD

Country	Capital	Form of State	Monetary Unit
Afghanistan	Kabul	Kingdom	Afghani
Albania	Tirana	Republic	Lek
Algeria	Algiers	Republic	Dinar
Andorra	Andorra La Vella	Republic	
Argentina	Buenos Aires	Republic	Peso
Australia	Canberra	*Dominion	Dollar
Austria	Vienna	Republic	Schilling
Barbados	Bridgetown	*	
Bahrain	Manama	Shaikhdom	Dinar
Belgium	Brussels	Kingdom	Belgian Franc
Bhutan	Punakha	Kingdom	
Bolivia	La Paz	Republic	Peso
Botswana	Gaberones	*	
Brazil	Brasilia	Republic	Cruzeiro
Bulgaria	Sofia	Republic	Lev
Burma	Rangoon	Republic	Kyat
Burundi	Bujumbura	Republic	B. Franc
Cambodia	Phnom Penh	Kingdom	Riel
Cameroon	Yaoundé	Republic	Franc C.F.A.
Canada	Ottawa	*Dominion	Dollar
Central African Republic	Bangui	Republic	
Ceylon	Colombo	Dominion	Rupee
Chad	Fort Lamy	Republic	
Chile	Santiago	Republic	Escudo
China	Peking	Republic	Jenminpi or Yuan
Colombia	Bogota	Republic	Peso
Congo	Brazzaville	Republic	
Congolese Republic	Kinshasa	Republic	Zaire
Costa Rica	San José	Republic	Colon
Cuba	Havana	Republic	Peso

* = member of the British Commonwealth

Country	Capital	Form of State	Monetary Unit
Cyprus	Nicosia	*Republic	C. Pound
Czechoslovakia	Prague	Republic	Koruna
Dahomey	Porto Novo	Republic	Franc C.F.A.
Denmark	Copenhagen	Kingdom	Krone
Dominican Republic	Ciudad Trujita	Republic	Peso
Ecuador	Quito	Republic	Sucre
Equatorial Guinea	Santa Isabel	Republic	
Ethiopia	Addis Ababa	Kingdom	E. Dollar
Finland	Helsinki	Republic	Markka
Formosa	Taipei	Republic	New Taiwan Dollar
France	Paris	Republic	Franc
Gabon	Libreville	Republic	Franc C.F.A.
Gambia	Bathurst	*	G. Pound
Germany, D.R.	East Berlin	Republic	Mark
Germany, Federal Rep.	Bonn	Republic	Deutsche Mark
Ghana	Accra	*Republic	Cedi
Greece	Athens	Kingdom	Drachma
Guatemala	Guatemala	Republic	Quetzal
Guyana	Georgetown	*Republic	G. Dollar
Guinea	Conakry	Republic	G. Franc
Haiti	Port au Prince	Republic	Gourde
Honduras	Tegucigalpa	Republic	Lempira
Hungary	Budapest	Republic	Forint
Iceland	Reykjavik	Republic	Krona
Irish Republic	Dublin	Republic	Pound
Italy	Rome	Republic	Lira
India	Delhi	*Republic	Rupee
Indonesia	Djakarta	Republic	Rupiah
Iran	Tehran	Kingdom	Rial
Iraq	Baghdad	Republic	Iraqui Dinar
Israel		Republic	Israel Pound
Ivory Coast	Abidjan	Republic	Franc C.F.A.
Jamaica	Kingston	*Dominion	J. Dollar
Japan	Tokyo	Kingdom	Yen
Jordan	Amman	Kingdom	J. Dinar
Kenya	Nairobi	*Republic	K. Shilling
Korea (North)	Pyongyang	Republic	Won
Korea (South)	Seoul	Republic	Won

Country	Capital	Form of State	Monetary Unit
Kuwait	Kuwait	Amirate	Kuwaiti Dinar
Laos	Vietiane	Kingdom	Kip
Lebanon	Beirut	Republic	L. Pound
Lesotho	Maseru	*Kingdom	
Liberia	Monrovia	Republic	L. Dollar
Libya	Beida	Republic	Libyan Pound
Liechtenstein	Vaduz	Principality	Swiss franc
Luxembourg	Luxembourg	Grand Duchy	Franc
Madagascar	Tananarive	Republic	Franc
Malawi	Zomba	Republic	M. Pound
Malaysia	Kuala Lumpur	*Kingdom	M. Dollar
Maldive Islands	Malé	Amirate	
Mali	Bamako	Republic	Franc Malien
Malta, G.C.	Valletta	*Ind-State	M. Pound
Mauritius	Port Louis	*Ind State	Rupee
Mauritania	Nouakchott	Republic	Franc C.F.A.
Mexico	Mexico City	Republic	Peso
Monaco	Monaco-ville	Principality	Franc
Mongolia	Ulan Bator	Republic	Tugrik
Morocco	Rabat	Kingdom	Dirham
Muscat and Oman	Muscat	Sultanate	Rupee
Nepal	Katmandu	Kingdom	Rupee
Netherlands	Hague	Kingdom	Florin
New Zealand	Wellington	*Dominion	N.Z. Dollar
Nicaragua	Managua	Republic	Cordoba
Niger	Niamey	Republic	Franc C.F.A.
Nigeria	Lagos	*	N. Pound
Norway	Oslo	Kingdom	Krone
Pakistan	{Islamabad, Rawalpindi	*Republic	Rupee
Panama	Panama City	Republic	Balboa
Paraguay	Asuncion	Republic	Guarani
Peru	Lima	Republic	Gold Sol
Philippines	Manila	Republic	Peso
Poland	Warsaw	Republic	Zloty
Portugal	Lisbon	Republic	Escudo
Rumania	Bucharest	Republic	Leu
Rwanda	Kigali	Republic	R. Franc
Salvador	San Salvador	Republic	Colon
San Marino	San Marino	Republic	
Saudi Arabia	Riyadh	Kingdom	Riyal

Country	Capital	Form of State	Monetary Unit
Senegal	Dakar	Republic	Franc C.F.A.
Sierra Leone	Freetown	*Dominion	Leone
Singapore		*Republic	S. Dollar
Somalia	Mogadishu	Republic	Somali
South Africa	Pretoria	Republic	Rand
S. Yemen	Aden	Republic	Dinar
Spain	Madrid	Republic	Peseta
Sudan	Khartoum	Republic	S. Pound
Swaziland	Mbabane	*Kingdom	
Sweden	Stockholm	Kingdom	Krona
Switzerland	Berne	Republic	Franc
Syria	Damascus	Republic	S. Pound
Tanzania	Dar-es-Salaam	*Republic	T. Shilling
Thailand (Siam)	Bangkok	Kingdom	Baht
Togo	Lomé	Republic	Franc C.F.A.
Tonga	Nukualofa	*Kingdom	Pa'anga
Trinidad and Tobago	Port of Spain	Dominion	T & T Dollar
Trucial States	Dubai	Shaikhdoms	Dinar
Tunisia	Tunis	Republic	Dinar
Turkey	Ankara	Republic	T. Pound
Uganda	Kampala	*Dominion	U. Shilling
United Arab Republic	Cairo	Republic	E. Pound
United Kingdom	London	*Kingdom	Pound
U.S.A.	Washington	Republic	Dollar
Upper Volta	Ouagadougou	Republic	Franc C.F.A.
Uruguay	Montevideo	Republic	Peso
U.S.S.R.	Moscow	Republic	Rouble
Venezuela	Caracas	Republic	Gold Bolivar
Vietnam N.	Hanoi	Republic	Dong
Vietnam S.	Saigon	Republic	Dong
Western Samoa	Apia	*	
Yemen	Taiz	Kingdom	Riyal
Yugoslavia	Belgrade	Republic	Dinar
Zambia	Lusaka	*Republic	Kwacha